Since 1995

HEAL THE HURT!
LIVE THE VICTORY!
The Workbook!

God's Spiritual, Mental, and Physical Transformation Seminar/Experience!

"For I will restore health unto thee, and I will heal thee of thy wounds, says the Lord;"
Jeremiah 30:17

"And the Lord said, Simon, Simon, behold, Satan hath desired to have you, that he may sift you as wheat: But I have prayed for thee, that thy faith fail not: and when thou art converted, strengthen thy brethren."
Luke 22:31-32

"Wherefore, my beloved, as ye have always obeyed, not as in my presence only, but now much more in my absence, work out your own salvation with fear and trembling."
Philippians 2:12

All scripture used herein is from the King James Version of the Holy Bible.

Please contact us!
Proof Positive Communications, Inc. @Facebook.com
The Institute for Christian Discipleship, Inc. @Facebook.com
icdbasics@gmail.com

A portion of the proceeds benefit
Institute for Christian Discipleship, Inc.
Sponsoring Churches
Non-Profit Ministries/Organizations when purchased in bulk.

DISCLAIMER!

The information contained in this workbook is provided through the divine inspiration of God the Holy Spirit. Faith in the God of Jesus Christ, the truth of Bible-based doctrine, and the success of participants in the ***Heal the Hurt! Live the Victory*** experience since 1992 is the only basis upon which this information is compiled and presented. No claims or guarantees are made regarding your success. Therefore, the author and the Institute for Christian Discipleship, Inc., its officers and Board of Directors shall be held blameless for the success of your participation, or progress.

Table of Contents

5.0 – VICTORY!

Beloved:

This letter brings to you our warmest personal greetings. On the wing, it bears our prayers for God's amazing grace to be showered in your life.

This workbook is dedicated to you and all who were wounded on the journey called life, and all who just want to improve their relationship with God, aggressively. You make a decision to be made whole through Jesus Christ, and improve your relationship with Him!

Therefore, thank you for including the work of God the Holy Spirit through The Institute for Christian Discipleship, Inc. into your faith journey. We know that your participation in **Heal the Hurt! Live the Victory** will bless you, as it continues to bless others and us.

Many who attended our seminars since 1992 requested this updated Workbook. It is designed to facilitate the manifestation of your healing, deliverance, and transformation. As God leads us, we use all possible means to share this simplistic, life-changing teaching that is based upon the Word of God. This workbook permits us to serve those who attend an actual seminar, as well as, those who participate through technology. We encourage you to eagerly embrace the systematic process for change that **The Workbook** provides.

God the Holy Spirit revealed the entire healing and deliverance process to the author as a result of sitting and visioning in the presence of God. The goal was to seek God for proactive ways to expand the original course, and more comprehensively advance the spiritual and emotional healing of as many people as possible, around the world. The same process is required for you to achieve your individual result from this study. Imagine yourself sitting with God the Holy Spirit who will "lead you into all truth".

Please accept our heartfelt thanks for your participation. The change you make, no matter how small will be magnificent. Change is inevitable. Intentional change is best. We know you will be an even greater witness of God's grace to others.

Grace and Peace,

Pastor Nawanna L. Miller – B.A., M.A., M.Div.
Founding Chairman and President

"... by His Grace!"

Foreword

Sons and Daughters of God:

"Heal the Hurt! Live the Victory!" is a seminar designed to address the hurt that both men and women often feel. To our detriment, the hurt controls our lives; and negates spiritual growth and victory in Christ Jesus.

Rev. Nawanna Miller attacks the issues of life with Biblical scripture that fortifies the believer, as he or she wrestles with the hurt, and God eventually liberates the saints from the pain. The Seminar is not simply catered to women, but to all of God's children. If you are in denial, or even unaware that you are hurting or have issues, Rev. Miller helps identify what it is that we feel.   Once clarity is established, she helps God to move you toward true purpose, which is to "Love and Worship God". She helps to steady the hurting or unsure believer in the shelter and security of God's Salvation. When we know we are anchored in the power of God's Salvation, we understand and believe that our destiny is a present and future reality through grace.

The Body of Christ is indebted to Rev. Miller who helps to plant us firmly in the security of the Father, through the salvific work of God the Son. However, be assured that although destiny is available, the believer must seek it and own it. In other words, it is no cheap grace. The participant must put in the work to be spiritually empowered as opposed to carnally led. Thus, we must "seek the Lord, while he may be found". If we are willing to seek, we will find.

Now, this seminar will do us no good, if we fail to be honest with the state of our lives, presently. Rev. Miller forces us to lift up the rug, to plunge the depths of our souls, and to wrestle with the real you. Once this is done, we can truly be healed and delivered.

This work is no small feat. Therefore, it should not be rushed. I highly recommend that seminar participants reserve at least five hours to this venture, with a lunch and after lunch session. Some things take time, and dealing with internal matters is weighty stuff.

Churches, pastors and certainly hurting people will benefit from this experience. Our church family sees people walk in victory as a result of the progressive nature of this work. You too will be blessed, if you allow this wonderful Seminar to be a part of the discipleship ministry of your church. Get healed, so that you may minister effectively in your community!

Love,

Rev. Dr. William E. Harris Jr. – B.A., M.Div., D.Min.
Pastor - Believers Christian Fellowship Church
Dayton, Ohio 45406

Scripture Matrix

It is written...

Romans 10:13-17

"For whosoever shall call upon the name of the Lord shall be saved. How then shall they call on him in whom they have not believed? And how shall they believe in him of whom they have not heard? And how shall they hear without a preacher? And how shall they preach, except they be sent? As it is written, How beautiful are the feet of them that preach the gospel of peace, and bring glad tidings of good things! But they have not all obeyed the gospel. For Isaiah saith, Lord, who hath believed our report? So then faith cometh by hearing, and hearing by the word of God."

Colossians 1:19-23

"For it pleased the Father that in him should all fullness dwell; And, having made peace through the blood of his cross, by him to reconcile all things unto himself; by him, I say, whether they be things in earth, or things in heaven. And you, that were sometime alienated and enemies in your mind by wicked works, yet now hath he reconciled in the body of his flesh through death, to present you holy and unblameable and unreproveable in his sight: If ye continue in the faith grounded and settled, and be not moved away from the hope of the gospel, which ye have heard, and which was preached to every creature which is under heaven; whereof I Paul am made a minister;

I John 4:15-19

"Whosoever shall confess that Jesus is the Son of God, God dwells in him, and he in God. And we have known and believed the love that God hath to us. God is love; and he that dwells in love dwells in God, and God in him. Herein is our love made perfect, that we may have boldness in the day of judgment: because as he is, so are we in this world. There is no fear in love; but perfect love casts out fear: because fear hath torment. He that fears is not made perfect in love. We love him, because he first loved us."

Hebrews 11:1

"Now faith is the substance of things hoped for, the evidence of things not seen."

TESTIMONY!

The moment I read the very first page in my workbook, I felt like I wanted to leap out of my seat! The familiar tears of my life began to swell, but this time...."*something*" (God) wouldn't let them fall. It was time to heal. I began to feel my own strength replacing past feelings of doubt and wanting to shut down! It seemed every word, every scripture, was written with me in mind! For many years, I struggled with life altering anxiety attacks that kept me in a serious holding pattern. I was unsure of myself because I had never been allowed to be myself.

You see, from early on in my life I was overly sheltered and often looked upon as "Too Pretty" or "Too Cute" to do anything. I didn't have to wash dishes or take out trash, no chores at all. Now this might not bother the average child, in fact one might be overjoyed. However, it wasn't long before "My Pretty" which I never saw in the first place became my place of burden.

I didn't want to be pretty... I didn't want to be spoiled because it seemed to me that it distanced me from my siblings. I kept asking myself for years, "What child asks to be spoiled?" I certainly didn't and though I enjoyed its rewards initially, it soon became a burden that I couldn't lift. Why?? I just didn't know how. Therefore, I suffered and withdrew into myself, cowering in the shadows of others. I gave up on being all that I could be because it was more important for me to make others happy instead of myself. So, I allowed anxiety to enter and comfortably welcomed fear along the way. They both held me hostage for over 50 years!!!

After attending the Heal the Hurt Seminar (Sessions I & II), I was able to look back over my life and to finally tackle those past hurts and disappointments that caused me so much pain. I was taught how to look at where my hurt began. Therefore, I was able to unclutter my mind, heart, and soul. Now that I am free, I can truthfully say I am moving on up in my life with Christ.

I will forever be grateful to Pastor Nawanna Lewis Miller and the Institute for Christian Discipleship for permitting God to use them in such a mighty way!

Veronica Long

I have taken the Heal the Hurt Seminar three times and would take it again. I say this because it has truly saved my life and has made me a better person. I take away something new each and every time I enroll in this class/seminar! Words cannot explain how I feel because of the things from which I have been delivered. There is nothing better in this world than being restored so that God can use us for His purpose. I encourage anyone who needs to be healed and delivered to take this wonderful opportunity to do so. You will be blessed beyond great measures.

Teisha Gayle

Introduction

In 1992, God the Holy Spirit gave The **Heal the Hurt! Live the Victory! Spiritual, Mental, Physical Transformation Seminar/Experience** to the author at Metropolitan Baptist Church in Washington, where Rev. Dr. H. Beecher Hicks, Jr. is Pastor. Since that time, God continues to reveal many new and exciting applications of Biblical truths, as a result of seminars and victories through the years.

The original version of this teaching was revised in 2007 and is now Seminar II. Seminar II is entitled **Heal the Hurt! Live the Victory! – 12 Keys to Spiritual Recovery.** This workbook concentrates on Seminar I, only, which was also added in 2007. Completion of these pages is the next step following your presence at one of our national seminars; participation through a Webinar; or as independent study with the PowerPoint presentation.

Together, the PowerPoint Presentation and this Workbook are systematic diagnostic tools, for your eyes only. Trust God the Holy Spirit who is the Teacher, to work with you to do your self-examination; and mend the broken places in your life. Please cooperate! (Smile!) Please watch the PowerPoint, first. Don't rush the process! Watch it again if necessary. Then, spend at least 40 minutes each day with your workbook and thoughts until completed. This is a process. Pray every step of the way.

To maximize the healing and deliverance of God the Holy Spirit, students are strongly encouraged to complete all components. There are no right or wrong answers. The answers are yours. Own them. Be honest with God and yourself. God already knows the truth better than we ever could. It is time to experience freedom from the past hurts, and live the abundant life that Jesus secured for you.

When you finish the Workbook, you are ready to engage in **Seminar II – Heal the Hurt! Live the Victory! – 12 Keys to Spiritual Recovery.** Upon verification of completion of Seminar I and Seminar II, you are eligible to become a Life Guardian. The role of the Life Guardian is to support a local, national and international network of Christians who are committed to remaining free in Jesus; and to facilitate the deliverance, healing, and recovery of others as we minister, daily. In Luke 22:31-32, Jesus commands Peter that when he is converted, when he is changed, to strengthen the brethren. Jesus commands us to do the same thing when we are converted or changed

The Gospel of Mark presents Jesus as the suffering servant who touched lives and changed circumstances on His way to the cross. Therefore, Jesus is our example that as we learn to walk in the healing of Isaiah 53:5, we realize the victory in Christ Jesus. We live out our conversion as we **stop, stoop, and lift** someone on our way to heaven.

You have power that you have not yet realized. Get free. Be free. Then, help God break the shackles off the lives of others.

CONTEMPLATIONS!

(Following are random excerpts from God the Holy Spirit that are included in my book entitled **Cruising the Cosmos!** Think on these things and all the scriptures, as you make your journey to new discovery and relationship with God.)

#1 – "Everything has changed! Every change has changed! Every change changes me!"

#2 – "Why is there an abandoned road? Is there no one who will prepare the way of the Lord? Why are His paths not made straight? Who is the soldier who is AWOL? Do we not know of His imminent return?"

#3 – "We are obligated as soldiers in the Army of the Lord to show up, every day that God sends, fit for duty. If that is true and the expectation of the King's Return is real, then sickness is not an option for us. God's Covenants are God's side of the agreement, fulfilled. Our side is to believe!"

#4 – True faith seeks ever-increasing revelation of God's truth and spiritual insight that lead to true worship of the True Triune God."

#5 – "Faith is the search for the matchless God in the midst of the ordinary. When the faith search is fully extended and engaged, it will lead us through the wilderness of uncertainty to the oasis in the desert places. There, in that place, the God of our salvation welcomes us into the Presence of His Knowing. In the Presence of His Knowing, Divine Truth is revealed to our minds, hearts, soul, and spirit."

#10 – "If we want something from God, we must step up our game. We must offer Isaac, the all and the best that we have, in sacrifice. When we offer Isaac, we do so whether there is a ram in the bush or not. That level of sacrifice brings us to the mountaintop of surrender that brings the ram into view. The ram was there all the time. Expect the ram. The ram is there. Worship follows that crosses the peaks of the mountain to greet the God of the Covenant, Creator of the ram and our room for escape."

#11 – "We humans are like moths, banging away in the darkness, seeking the Light, until we discover God's abiding Presence and Guiding Radiance within."

#15 – "Double-mindedness leads to double vision, staggered steps, duality of personality, ambivalent affection toward God, and ultimately self-destructive behavior called sin."

#17 – "Prayer is God's provision for us to flow on the current of grace beyond the veil, into the Presence of God. God desires that we come into His Presence. In God's Presence, we know that the shadow of the Almighty keeps us. In the Presence, every need is provided. Every truth is available. Every question is already answered."

GOD IS... THAT'S ENOUGH!

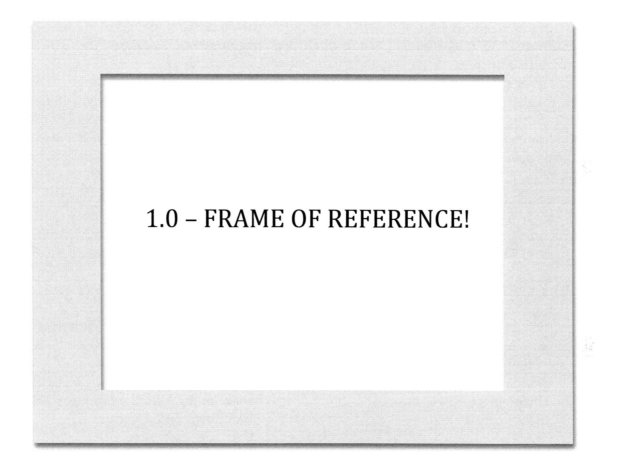

1.0 – FRAME OF REFERENCE!

1.1 – HISTORICAL PERSPECTIVE

Leviticus 19:18 – "Thou shalt not avenge, nor bear any grudge against the children of thy people, but thou shalt love thy neighbor as thyself: I am the Lord."

Deuteronomy 6:4 – "Hear, O Israel: The Lord our God is one Lord:

Matthew 22:37-40 – "Jesus said unto him, Thou shalt love the Lord thy God with all thy heart, and with all thy soul, and with all thy mind. This is the first and great commandment. And the second is like unto it, Thou shalt love thy neighbor as thyself. On these two commandments hang all the law and the prophets."

Hypothesis: If we are obedient to the First and Great Commandment, and the Second Commandment that Jesus gave, if we get these two correctly, God empowers us to obey all other commandments. We will stand in faith and obedience to the commandments of God, on God's promises, and live the abundant life. God will use us as living testimonies through our systematic study and change.

Think on These Things!

- God gave Moses the Ten Commandments according to Exodus 20.

- God gave 613 more commandments that are based upon the first Ten (10).

- Jesus summarized the 613 Commandments – all the Law and the Prophets – into two Commandments that instruct us to love God; love ourselves; and love our neighbor.

- Obedience to these two Commandments is essential for followers of Jesus Christ to live the life of obedience, holiness, service, abundance, and reward.

- There is a difference in knowing what the Bible says, and living what God commands.

- Obedience to the two Commandments is not optional.

- God the Holy Spirit makes it possible to obey the Commandments.

- The Bible is God's Covenant/Agreement with us. It is the blueprint for LIFE!

- Is it possible that you are attempting to follow Christ without giving your full attention to the First/Great and Second Commandments?

Problem Statement: How can we obey Matthew 22:37-40 if:

1. Love of God and the will of God are not our exclusive first priority;
2. Our hearts are broken;
3. Forgiveness is refused (even of ourselves);
4. Our minds are in disarray;
5. A root of bitterness and other unhealthy roots exist in our hearts;
6. Our souls are scattered to the wind because we are yet attached to so many things and people from our past or present that are unhealthy;
7. We fail to see ourselves and others through the eyes of Christ; OR
8. We are uncertain of our relationship with Jesus Christ?

Deuteronomy 6:4 is called the Shema. The Shema is the confession of faith for the Hebrew or Jewish people. The name for the confession is derived from the first word, Shema (Hear). God gave Moses the Shema to give to the people who were required to recite it every morning when they arose and every evening when they laid down to go to sleep. That is good prayer practice that yields results!

The purpose of the Shema is to declare that Jehovah – God – is the only True God. It also includes Deuteronomy 11:13-21 and Numbers 15:37-41. The Shema is a reminder of the Ten Commandments, the first four of which declare the absolute sovereignty of the True God. God required the Israelites and us to be monotheistic – worshippers of One God who we now know is the Trinity. We worship the Trinity – the Three in One God!

Write Deuteronomy 11:13 below.

_____

_____

_____

_____

_____

List the promises God makes to you in Deuteronomy 11:14-15.

_____

_____

_____

_____

_____

Describe what the warning for disobedience means in Deuteronomy 11:16-17.

_____

_____

_____

_____

List the instructions for following the Commandments in Deuteronomy 11:18-20.

_____

_____

_____

_____

What is the benefit of obedience that Deuteronomy 11:21 specifies?

_____

_____

_____

_____

When we look at the First and Great Commandment, and the Second Commandment, we see that Jesus restates the commands from the Old Testament Scriptures mentioned on these two pages.

Therefore, the answer to the Problem Statement is that it impossible to obey the First and Great Commandment or the Second, if any one of the conditions of #'s 1-8 in the Problem Statement exists in our lives. It is pretty much guaranteed that at least one exists or as many as all eight of the conditions exist in the lives of people. The Old Testament reveals that to us, and they received the instructions 1450 years before Christ arrived. Over two thousand years after the Resurrection and Ascension of Christ, and Pentecost, God yet commands us in Matthew 22:37-40 to be obedient to the summary of all the Law and the Prophets. What could be the challenges to our obedience?

For the work sessions in which you are about to engage, you are encouraged to see life through the metaphor of a picture frame. A photo of you captures certain features and locks it in time. However, it does not portray what transpired in your life. Keep the Shema and Matthew 22:37-40 in your mind and spirit as you look at "you" through your frame of reference.

1.2 – WHAT IS YOUR PERSONAL FRAME OF REFERENCE?

Briefly make comments about YOU (your essence, journey, history, etc.).

_____

_____

_____

_____

_____

_____

Describe which comment above is the most significant in how you see yourself.

_____

_____

_____

_____

How do you feel about yourself when you are alone?

_____

_____

_____

1.3 – RE-FRAME!

There comes a point in time when even the best portrait needs a new frame. So it is with life. We should be deliberate, intentional and aggressive to re-frame our lives and our points of view to see ourselves through the eyes of Christ, the way that God sees us. To do so requires honest, spiritual assessment. Please complete the following.

1. On a scale from 1-10, (1 is lowest – 10 highest) honestly assess how well you line up with "these two Commandments" in Matthew 22:37-40. Please circle one (1) for each statement.

   a) I Love God with ALL my heart!

          1   2   3   4   5   6   7   8   9   10

   b) I love God with ALL my soul!

          1   2   3   4   5   6   7   8   9   10

   c) I love God with my entire mind!

          1   2   3   4   5   6   7   8   9   10

   d) I love myself!!

          1   2   3   4   5   6   7   8   9   10

   e) I love God through love for my neighbor as I love myself!

          1   2   3   4   5   6   7   8   9   10

2. What do you desire God to change in your life for you to align with the New Testament's First/Great and Second Commandments? Keep it simple!

_____

_____

_____

_____

_____

1.4 – SELF-ASSESSMENT!

Verbally repeat Isaiah 53:5. As you respond to the following, please give each one to Jesus for removal.

Identify three (3) of your current transgressions for which Jesus was wounded.

1) _____

2) _____

3) _____

Identify three (3) of your iniquities (tendencies toward sin, sin-diseases, habits, frailties, weaknesses, etc.) for which Jesus was bruised on His way to the cross.

1) _____

2) _____

3) _____

Identify three (3) areas of peace that you desire to receive or currently possess that Jesus secured for you on His way to the cross.

1) _____

2) _____

3) _____

Identify a physical, spiritual, and an emotional healing that you know the stripes of Jesus secured for you on His way to the cross.

1) _____

2) _____

3) _____

Identify three (3) habits or sin-dis-eases in your life from which you need deliverance and healing.

1) _____

2) _____

3) _____

Identify three (3) habits or sin dis-eases from which God has already delivered and healed you.

1) _____

2) _____

3) _____

Isaiah 55:11 – "So shall my word be that goeth forth out of my mouth: it shall not return unto me void, but it shall accomplish that which I please, and it shall prosper in the thing whereto I sent it."

Based upon Isaiah 55:11, please write a brief commentary about the power of the Word of God for the manifestation of your healing and wholeness!

_____

_____

_____

_____

How will you walk in that truth as your reality?

_____

_____

_____

_____

REMEMBER! The Word of God has all power within Itself to get "Itself" done.

1.5 – SPIRITUAL ENERGY AUDIT!

The utility companies make an energy audit of our homes available to consumers to see where heat or air escape. What if we did an energy audit of our spiritual lives? Where does the power of God the Holy Spirit escape from us?

God requires us to be good stewards of all resources and assets. God also requires us to give a minimum of 10% of our time, talent, and treasure to the work of the Kingdom of God. The following Spiritual Energy Audit will indicate where there is seepage of spiritual energy or waste. As a result of this process, you should facilitate the changes in your life to eliminate loss and future hindrances to continuous spiritual maturity. When you finish the audit, compare what you do for you to what you do for God, daily. It will probably be very interesting. Smile!

Regular Activities	Hours / Day	Hours / Week
Working		
Transporting or Working w/Children/ Family /Friends		
Sleeping		
Television (News, Shows, Sports)		
Eating		
Commuting		
Cooking		
Exercise		
Reading (Articles / Books)		
Surfing the Internet		
Facebook / Web Conversations		
Entertainment (Games, Movies, etc.)		
Shower / Bath		
Cleaning / Repairing the Home		

Grocery Shopping		
Styling Hair, Barber Shop, Shaving		
Dressing		
Talking on Telephone (Business, Social, etc.)		
Organizing		
Automobile (Gas, washing, etc.)		
Talking Politics/TV News/Sports/Television		
Shopping / Window Shopping		
Texting		
Hobby (Golf, Tennis, Cards. Basketball)		
Socializing		
Drinking, Gambling, Smoking, Lottery		
Meetings / Networking		
Setting Goals / Planning		
Grieving the Past		
List Others:		
Total		

Daily Bible-Based Actions	Hours / Day	Hours / Week
Personal Prayer w/o Ceasing (Eph. 6:18; 1 Thess. 5:17)		
Corporate Prayer (Acts 1:14; 1:24; 4:31; 6:6; 13:3; 14:23; 21:5)		
Personal Bible Study (2 Timothy 2:15)		
Corporate Bible Study (2 Timothy 2:15)		
Personal Worship (2 Timothy 2:15)		
Corporate Worship (Psalms 99; 100, 138; John 1:4; Acts 1-28; Heb.12; 13)		
Discipleship (Matt. 10)		
Missions/Service to Others (Matt. 25:34-46)		
Evangelism (Matt. 28:18-20)		
Demonstrations of Love (John 3:16; Luke 6:27-36)		
Stewarding the Church Facilities/Ministries (Matt. 20; I Cor. 4:1-2)		
Casting out Demons (Luke 10:19; 2 Tim. 1:7)		
Deliverance of Others (Luke 4:18-27)		
Edifying Others (I Cor. 14:5)		
Using Spiritual Gifts & Talents (I Cor. 12; Eph. 4:12-16)		
List Others:		
Total		

1.6 – FRAME OF REFERENCE FOR DIMENSIONS!

From a spiritual point of view, "science is seeing God through God's creation", according to what God revealed to this writer many years ago. We most assuredly know that the vastness of God is unlimited; and beyond human ability to discover all of who God is and what God created. We believe the Word. Through a process of discovery only, not creation, science initiates a sometimes complex explanation of what God created and how. The discoveries of science will forever remain incomplete, yet we are indebted to scientists. We are often reluctant to accept scientific facts. The interesting thing is that through the ages many who sought to use science to discredit God discover and accept Jesus Christ as Lord and Savior of their lives, as a result of their research. We benefit. God is still God!

With those thoughts in mind, around 1995, astrophysicists advanced a theory that there are at least 11 dimensions in our physical universe. It is called the **M-Theory or String Theory** (sometimes called the **U-Theory**). Until then, we acknowledged only four dimensions – space, time, height, and depth. From a scientific point of view, there is much debate over the **M Theory**.

What God says in the Bible needs no proof. However, through the **M-Theory** or **String Theory**, God the Holy Spirit opens the door to knowledge and understanding. Through physics, God reveals a portion, only a portion, of the mystery of God's Omnipresence – God's ability to be everywhere at the same time.

The truth that humans are unable to discover with intellect alone is that there are probably more dimensions than can ever be counted. What we do know is that God is Omnipresent – everywhere at the same time – though not in everything.

Begin **End**

This diagram simply shows that we travel in time on a straight line, with a start and end point. Humans can only move forward in the space/time dimension, not backwards. Yet, neither the space/time dimension nor height nor depth can limit God. God is able to move in any dimension or direction at any time, according to God's will.

Jesus, the Author and Finisher of our faith wrote our story (Hebrews 12:2), and handled every detail before the foundation of the world. According to John 1, Jesus, the Triune God, completed everything, in the beginning. When we accept Jesus as Lord and Savior, He enters into relationship with us, and walks with us through the journey of life to the finish line. Eternal life continues. You are so important to God that God sent His Son to die in your place. Let's live the Christ-Life that Jesus secured and guarantees for us. Jesus likes what He wrote about us. Let's seek to know and believe THAT story through the Word of God.

Please go back to **Image 1.6.** Draw 11 horizontal lines and 11 vertical lines. Choose one horizontal line and make it darker than the others. That's your lifeline. Place a dot on the line within any square you choose. That dot represents you. Jesus is there with you, wherever you go; and everywhere else at the same time. (Smile!) Jesus is unlimited. He walked through closed doors on earth, and transcended at His will. Remember this! While humans are only able to move forward in time, the space/time dimension does not limit God's movement. Therefore, God is able to move between dimensions, which probably far exceed the 11 that are discovered.

The Laws of Physics help us to see the Power of God's Omnipresence. Wherever you are in your journey, God is! Jesus promised that He would never leave you nor forsake you! Go forward. Don't stop or give up. Those issues and people who held you in spiritual bondage can hurt you no more. Let go! Live in new dimensions, unlimited dimensions – not just at another level in the same dimension. Opportunities for new blessings wait for you, as you obey and prepare through study, prayer and preparation to receive those opportunities.

It is written:

Exodus 14:13-15 – "And Moses said unto the people, fear ye not, stand still, and see the salvation of the Lord, which he will shew you today: for the Egyptians whom ye have seen today, ye shall see them no more forever. The Lord shall fight for you, and ye shall hold your peace. And the Lord said unto Moses, Wherefore criest thou unto me? speak unto the children of Israel, that they go forward:"

Egyptians can represent people, or situations that hindered or hurt you in the past or present. What does God's command to "go forward" mean to you regarding your hurt?

_____

_____

_____

_____

_____

It is written:

Matthew 28:20 – "lo I am with you always, even to the end of the world. Amen."

How does the truth that God is everywhere at the same time comfort you, based on the Bible, the String Theory, and the existence of at least 11 dimensions?

_____

_____

_____

_____

Please read Hebrews 12:1-2, again. Imagine Jesus writing your story of salvation before the foundation of the world! Apparently, He loved what He wrote about you because Jesus loves you. So, you should love God and yourself, too. Through this workbook, you simply make edits in your story because life brought, and yet brings things that you don't need to keep. Yet, God transforms the past for God's best good for your life. Provisions are already in place for you.

God the Holy Spirit walks with you to finish your story. When Jesus said, "It is finished" that included you and everything pertaining to you. It's "all good"! Smile!

What good thoughts do you think God thought towards you, when your story was written? Please write them below! Glorify God through celebration of God in you!

_____

_____

_____

_____

_____

_____

_____

Write a Prayer of Thanksgiving for the original love-story Jesus wrote about you!

_____

_____

_____

_____

_____

_____

_____

_____

_____

_____

_____

1.7 – PRAY!

DON'T LISTEN TO OR USE MERELY BUZZ WORDS ABOUT YOUR GOD AND YOUR FAITH IN JESUS CHRIST! OUR GOD IS VASTLY GREATER THAN CLICHES! WOULD YOU JUST SAY WHAT EVERY ONE ELSE SAYS ABOUT SOMEONE THAT YOU LOVE OR WOULD YOU USE YOUR OWN DESCRIPTION?

Prayer is a two-way conversation with God who has the answer to absolutely everything. Don't just talk to God! LISTEN TO GOD! Buzz Words, on the other hand, are common, overused, impersonal expressions from someone else that others just start to repeat and use. GOD WANTS ORIGINAL, PERSONAL CONVERSATIONS WITH US!

Buzz Words are just that. They create a buzz – common point of conversation – everyone's saying it. The challenge to our life-change is to know what God says to us personally through prayer and through God's Holy Word.

Below, please write your own words or adjectives to describe your personal relationship/experience with God. (Say something other than "God is Good".)

_____

_____

_____

_____

_____

1.8 – WHAT DID JESUS SAY?

John 3:3-8 – "Jesus answered and said unto him, Verily, verily, I say unto thee, except a man be born again, he cannot see the kingdom of God. Nicodemus saith unto him, how can a man be born when he is old? Can he enter the second time into his mother's womb, and be born? Jesus answered, Verily, verily, I say unto thee, except a man be born of water and of the Spirit, he cannot enter into the kingdom of God. That which is born of the flesh is flesh; and that which is born of the Spirit is spirit. Marvel not that I said unto thee, ye must be born again. The wind blows where it listeth, and thou heareth the sound thereof, but canst not tell whence it cometh, and whither it goeth: so is every one that is born of the Spirit."

1 Peter 1:23 – "Being born again, not of corruptible seed, but of incorruptible, by the word of God, which lives and abides for ever."

Regeneration or Rebirth is the PROCESS through which God the Holy Spirit makes us new creatures by the incorruptible seed of God's Word. Rebirth or regeneration requires us to know, do and live what the Word of God says pertaining to us.

We pray fervent prayers for new revelations based on the Word of God. God speaks most often through the Holy Scriptures, though not exclusively. The scriptures always validate what God says through any other medium (form of communication) God chooses to use to talk to us.

REMEMBER! God can save us instantly. However, we didn't form as a sinner in a flash. So, the REBIRTH is a process that requires our active engagement with God the Holy Spirit to remove old things. Stay calm! Be patient with God and yourself!

Write a brief commentary on what John 3:3-16 means to your life in Christ.

_____

_____

_____

_____

_____

_____

_____

_____

_____

Examine the following scriptures. What does God say to you through them?

John 18:31-32

_____

_____

Psalm 32:8

_____

_____

Proverbs 3:25-26

_____

_____

_____

James 5:14-15

_____

_____

_____

Hebrews 10:35-37

_____

_____

_____

John 11:25-26

_____

_____

_____

1.9 – ABOUT PURPOSE!

Purpose is one of the Buzz Words that everyone uses!

Our PURPOSE is to love, worship and serve
God in Spirit and in Truth!

Stop chasing windmills! Follow God's
Plan!
Jeremiah 29:11

2 Kings 5:1-4 – "Now Naaman, captain of the host of the king of Syria, was a great man with his master, and honorable, because by him the LORD had given deliverance unto Syria: he was also a mighty man in valor, but he was a leper. And the Syrians had gone out by companies, and had brought away captive out of the land of Israel a little maid; and she waited on Naaman's wife. And she said unto her mistress, would to God my lord were with the prophet that is in Samaria for he would recover him of his leprosy. And one went in, and told his lord, saying, thus and thus said the maid that is of the land of Israel."

Which character are you in the story of Naaman? Are you the person who is well known like Naaman who has received great accolades, yet you're a spiritual leper? Or are you the one who has the answers that someone else needs to be healed?

At some level, we are both.   As a Born-Again Christian, we are Naaman who is immensely powerful.   However, in some ways we are lepers because we are yet burdened by something, hiding something or hiding from something. We must get to Jesus! Jesus will take the bandages off our wounded places and reveal the healing, deliverance, and recovery that He already secured for us.

In the spirit, we are the peasant girl who has the answer for someone else's healing, according to the Word of God. Remember what Jesus told Peter to do when he was converted? Start talking about Jesus. Someone, a great leader or an uncelebrated individual (according to human standards) needs to hear the Truth. As a result of his healing, verse 15 says it all. Naaman worshipped the true God.

"And he returned to the man of God, he and all his company, and came, and stood before him: and he said, Behold, *now I know that there is no God in all the earth, but in Israel*: now therefore, I pray thee, take a blessing of thy servant."

Our purpose is to love God with all our heart, soul, and mind – to be filled fully with God the Holy Spirit, at all times. That Agape (love) yields true worship of God that includes giving. If we understand that, then, we follow our God-given passion, as Born-Again Christians. If we do the will of God, we worship because we can't help but worship. Healing from God will flow in us and for us; then through us, to someone else.

I recommend that you read or re-read **The Practice of the Presence of God** by Brother Lawrence who died February 12, 1691. It is a small book about a devout man who fulfilled his life's purpose of worship in a monastery doing simple chores as unto the Lord! He served! He used the Gift of Helps in ordinary ways. His simple story of worship changed countless lives. He teaches us that to get in the presence of God to worship and serve on purpose is the victory of holiness in Christ Jesus. Brother Lawrence's letters and memoirs form the book that has sold millions of copies over the course of three centuries, and are yet selling. He understood purpose as the worship of God through service. He yet blesses millions.

Remember Naaman! Write a brief commentary on how to connect with the power and presence of God, both in your corporate worship and alone. Practice that!

_____

_____

_____

_____

How do you expect your worship to change as a result of healing your hurt?

_____

_____

_____

_____

What do you passionately desire to do NOW or as your life's work that will glorify God and generate more reverence in your personal and corporate worship?

_____

_____

_____

_____

_____

Identify the specific goals and objectives that you have set to live out your passion for Christ and use your Spiritual Gifts as an act of worship?

_____

_____

_____

_____

_____

_____

_____

True worship helps us to resist the enemy's attacks and prevent new hurt. What steps have you taken OR will you take to live a lifestyle of worship going forward?

_____

_____

_____

_____

_____

Proverbs 19:21 – "Many are the plans in a man's heart, but it is the Lord's purpose that prevails."

1.10 – ABOUT DESTINY!

"Live the Christ-Life as a Fenced City in the Salvation of the Son of God!"

Destiny is another Buzz Word. For the sons and daughters of God through Jesus Christ, our destiny IS the salvation of Jesus Christ, now and forever. Ultimately, our final destination is eternal life in heaven. Eternity begins here with heaven on earth! It is written:

Ephesians 1:3-4 – "Blessed be the God and Father of our Lord Jesus Christ, who hath blessed us with all spiritual blessings in heavenly places in Christ: According as he hath chosen us in him before the foundation of the world, that we should be holy and without blame before him in love…"

In laboring for understanding of the word destiny, God the Holy Spirit gave the author the sentence above in a night vision. God said: "Live the Christ-Life as a fenced city in the Salvation of the Son of God." That was all. It was enough!

Read Exodus 27. In that chapter, God gave instructions for building the fence that was to surround the Tabernacle. The Tabernacle in the Old Testament is a typology or prefiguring of Christ who is revealed in the New Testament. In the Old Testament, the fence separated the Tabernacle or the dwelling place of God, from the world. It separated the holy from the unholy. God says: "Separate the holy things unto Me, including your life, from the unholy things of this world."

The fence represents how Jesus separates us from the world and its harm. Through the power of His Presence in our lives, we are separated in the salvation of Jesus Christ unto holiness. We are called to holiness!

In that night vision, God revealed once more that Jesus Christ made all provisions for us in salvation – our destiny. The search is over. We simply work with God the Holy Spirit to embrace and believe all that is included in our destiny that is salvation. God says we are a fenced city. Faith and obedience are the electrified security to keep us safe/saved. (Seminar II expands on the Doctrine of Salvation.)

Imagine! You have been on a long journey without understanding most or any of the directions you were to follow. You finally arrive at your destination and feel totally secure and confident that this is the place you were headed all along, but didn't know it. Live the life of peace, knowing you live in your destiny – salvation.

Don't buy into the perpetual search that the BUZZWORD called destiny requires. YOU ARE NOT LOST LOOKING FOR DESTINY if you are saved! Because of the Christ of the cross, our destiny is secure in Him. God chose us for salvation in Jesus Christ (Destiny) before the foundation of the world. Take the pressure off! Enjoy the trip. Pack only what you need. Dump the rest!

Notice the details of God in Exodus 27:9-18. In your own words, how do you relate it to God's details about your destiny IN the salvation of Jesus Christ?

_____

_____

_____

_____

_____

Describe what Revelation 21:3 means to you regarding your destiny – salvation!

_____

_____

_____

Luke 22:31-32 - "And the Lord said, Simon, Simon, behold, Satan hath desired to have you, that he may sift you as wheat: But I have prayed for thee, that thy faith fail not: and when thou art converted (changed), strengthen thy brethren."

Based on Luke 22:31-32 and Revelation 21:3, explain why YOUR continuous change is necessary as Peter's was necessary for him?

_____

_____

_____

_____

What do you see and sense in your spirit in the salvation place called Destiny?

_____

_____

_____

_____

_____

_____

What decision will you make to enjoy this new life?

_____

_____

_____

_____

_____

You have arrived at your destiny – SALVATION! Practice living your life there with eternity in your view until you arrive! Stop the struggle and the mind games to get to some place in life. Rise up! Live abundantly! The search is over! God values you! You are blessed!

Throughout your process of study, you will see how important imagination and visioning are to heal your hurts, strengthen your weaknesses, and achieve your goals for the victorious life Jesus already provided. Stretch your thoughts to reveal God's revelation and enhance your imagination. Take the self-imposed limits off your life. You will be amazed!

"A Mighty Fortress is Our God!"

1.11 - YOU ARE SAFE!
Stay inside God's Spiritual Fortress of Salvation!

Nahum 1:7 – "The Lord is good, a strong hold in the day of trouble; and he knows them that trust in him."

God is our stronghold. Imagine yourself in the deep recesses of the fortress in this image with the Blood Covering of Jesus. We are SAFER than that in the salvation of Jesus Christ. When we live in that dimension of faith, we are secure – IN ALL THINGS! We have to work at believing that. Fear and doubt are our enemies. Mark 5:36 says: "Be not afraid. Only believe."

A Mighty Fortress is Our God is a significant hymn of The Church of Jesus Christ. It was a song of worship and triumph for Martin Luther during the Protestant Reformation, most commonly dated as beginning in 1517. The words to this hymn describe what it means to live in the strong hold of God that the scriptures describe.

Below, list at least three things you fear the most, which are holding you hostage. Pray and declare your faith and victory in Jesus Christ over them. Then slowly read or sing, aloud, the words to the hymn of our faith that follows. Encourage yourself and others in psalms, hymns and spiritual songs as Ephesians 5:19 requires!

_____

_____

A Mighty Fortress is Our God!
Text: Martin Luther
Trans. by Frederick H. Hedge

List Simple Thoughts about
Each Verse!

1.   A mighty fortress is our God,
a bulwark never failing;
our helper he amid the flood
of mortal ills prevailing.
For still our ancient foe
doth seek to work us woe;
his craft and power are great,
and armed with cruel hate,
on earth is not his equal.

2.   Did we in our own strength confide,
our striving would be losing,
were not the right man on our side,
the man of God's own choosing.
Dost ask who that may be?
Christ Jesus, it is he;
Lord Sabaoth, his name,
from age to age the same,
and he must win the battle.

3.   And though this world, with devils
filled, should threaten to undo us.
We will not fear, for God hath willed
his truth to triumph through us.
The Prince of Darkness grim,
we tremble not for him;
his rage we can endure,
for lo, his doom is sure;
one little word shall fell him.

4.   That word above all earthly powers,
no thanks to them, abideth;
the Spirit and the gifts are ours,
thru him who with us sideth.
Let goods and kindred go,
this mortal life also;
the body they may kill;
God's truth abideth still;
his kingdom is forever.

It is written:

Mark 9:29 - "And he said unto them, this kind can come forth by nothing, but by prayer and fasting."

2 Corinthians 10:4 - "(For the weapons of our warfare are not carnal, but mighty through God to the pulling down of strong holds;)"

Prayer, fasting and spiritual weapons are required for spiritual warfare. They are critical to the Christ-Life. As in most things, the enemy seeks to counterfeit the truth of God and prevent us from pressing into deliverance, recovery, and victory. One such example of the counterfeit is the stronghold. Issues of life that are not properly filtered through the Word of God and released to God can facilitate the establishment of the strongholds of the enemy in our lives without our knowledge. In other words, the previous image of the Mighty Fortress of our God has a counterfeit from the enemy. Here is how the counterfeit is used against us.

- Instead of remaining in the stronghold of God, the Mighty Fortress, many Christians seek to live the Christ-Life without knowing that somewhere in their environment the enemy set up an oppressive, counterfeit stronghold.

- Some personality traits that we either don't consider, or dismiss as a fact of life may be the portal/gateway the enemy enters to set up strongholds in our lives. (Examples: shyness, fearful, needy, aggressive, addictive behavior, spoiled, driven, shop-a-holic, work-a-holic, sad, angry, excessively boisterous, passive, complacent, melancholy, doubtful, etc.).

- Past hurts, unresolved issues, bitterness, shame, sorrow, etc. can actually become strongholds of the enemy that are used against us.

- If you use or hear others use a phrase like this – "I have always been this way", OR "I've been this way all my life", that is a spirit talking. It is probably speaking from a stronghold. God requires change – conversion!

- For the Born-Again Christian, daily, prayerful change is commanded.

If you are ready for release to move forward, then examine your life – past & present. Identify any strongholds of the enemy that you see or suspect are present, attempting to set up, or were removed and left a residue. If it's not God, it is self or satan!

_____

_____

_____

_____

What kinds of things/people continue to cause you distress or to respond in an angry or negative way? Please use single words. They signify conditions favorable for an enemy stronghold to set up. Spiritually change how you respond.

_____

_____

_____

_____

When the stronghold first began to set up, you were either unaware or felt powerless over the forces of darkness. Through our Lord Jesus Christ, God the Holy Spirit gives us access to the power of God. Describe your commitment to fasting and prayer as a weapon of warfare to work with God the Holy Spirit to pull down the enemy's strongholds in your life.

_____

_____

_____

_____

_____

What will you do to be watchful and prevent the set-up of future strongholds?

_____

_____

_____

_____

Please read Matthew 12:28-45. How will you add Biblical truths and Christ-centered behavior to that space in your life that was once a stronghold?

_____

_____

_____

_____

1.12 – WHO/WHAT CONTROLS YOUR LIFE? GOD? YOU? OR A RAG-A-MUFFIN LIKE THIS?

The Christ-Life requires our total surrender to the God of Jesus Christ who is the Supreme Authority. In the natural, humans often seek to CONTROL everything. In the natural state, some of us place ourselves on the throne of our lives, and leave God out of our decision-making. Then, we beg God to help us when things go wrong. We make plans and decisions then pray – consulting God after the fact. We bring God up to date in our little way, as we plead for help. Get you and your past out of God's seat. Move you out of God's way. Let God lead you to a victorious, peaceful, free place. Consider the following!

- Nature vs. Spirit – By nature or acting in the natural is the way we lived in the past. Spiritual is the way we live as the born-again sons and daughters of God. Change in heart, soul, and mind are required.

- Self-Led vs. God-Led – Self-led people make decisions without God. God-led saints pray first to consult God, and read the Word of God to seek God's will at all times.

- Carnal Christian vs. Spiritual Christian – Carnal Christians acknowledge or make a confession of Christ, but still live a worldly lifestyle. Little to no continuous Godly change is evident. Spiritual Christians live a lifestyle that reflects their relationship with Christ, at all times. They live a changed life. Spiritual Christians mortify (intentionally kill off) the flesh or the old natural person who will not die willingly on it's own like old habits, old fears, regrets, defeat, etc.

- A controlling spirit is an ungodly, carnal spirit. It often uses emotional tactics to obtain the desired result, even against God's will.

- Intellect vs. Divine Mind – Intellect says we can learn enough from life, books, etc. to live a blessed life. However, we must receive and depend on the Divine Mind of Christ that Christ makes available to the Born-Again.

The question is real and should be answered on a regular basis. Who/what is in charge of or controls your life?

_____

_____

_____

_____

_____

In the past, who or what determined how you made decisions and took action?

_____

_____

_____

_____

Romans 8:13 – "For if ye live after the flesh, ye shall die: but if ye through the   Spirit do mortify the deeds of the body, ye shall live."

How will you kill the fleshly desires and deeds to give God complete control, and live victoriously?

_____

_____

_____

_____

_____

_____

Repeat the following scripture in your mind; your heart; and then aloud!

Colossians 3:5 – "Mortify therefore your members which are upon the earth; fornication, uncleanness, inordinate affection, evil concupiscence, and covetousness, which is idolatry:"

The hurts, sin-dis-eases or habits formed in the past will not leave willingly. Our diligent efforts to work with God the Holy Spirit must be applied to remove them from our lives. God perfects whatever we surrender to God!

In the context of Colossians 3:5, describe the sin dis-eases, behavior, or iniquity (your personal tendency toward sin) that you will intentionally destroy immediately, and forever through the power of God the Holy Spirit.

_____

_____

_____

_____

_____

_____

_____

_____

_____

_____

_____

_____

What will you do to reflect God's authority in your daily lifestyle, going forward?

_____

_____

_____

_____

A spirit of control can often be the result of a covetous spirit, which is idolatry.

1.13 – QUESTION TO CONSIDER DAILY!

Are you living your life from a junk drawer?
Cute on the outside… Clutter on the inside?

In which specific areas does your interior life and Bible-based beliefs need to match up with your attractive, successful, exterior appearance?

_____

_____

_____

_____

_____

_____

_____

_____

1.14 – HOW DOES YOUR SPIRITUAL LIFE LOOK?
Are you an emotional/spiritual hoarder?

Look at each image. Think about the function of each one. Circle all that apply to you and hoarding. Imagine you are trapped in that circle with each thing you hoard. Write a simple, one word description near the image that describes what it means to you. Have fun! Doodle or draw your own and add words.

1.15 – COULD THIS BE YOU?
Are you spiritually/emotionally buried alive?

Could this be your spiritual, emotional, and/or physical self? Spiritual or emotional hoarders hold on to things, experiences, and people that no longer are beneficial to their lives. Spiritual hoarding begins with one thing at a time to which a false value is assigned. It can ultimately produce an internal landfill in the heart, soul, mind, spirit or body. Imagine this waste anywhere inside of you!

However, some valuable truths, skills, experiences, visions, ideas, etc. are hidden in this landfill that can represent your life's journey that you should keep. There are also MANY things that need to be discarded. Think through the interior of your life and ask God the Holy Spirit to extract the valuable and discard the rest. Make room for new spiritual growth, new ideas, and new blessings.

Think of the shovel on the end as magnetic with the power to remove the good. As you can see, only a few articles are on the shovel in the image. God the Holy Spirit works with you to select what is valuable from the junk pile of your life experience. Keep that. It is used as a part of your re-framing, and to change your life for God's glory and your good.

It is written

Matthew 7:14 – "Because strait is the gate, and narrow is the way, which leadeth unto life, and few there be that find it."

BOTTOM LINE! You can't take the excess baggage with you through the narrow way "unto life". Just like taking an airplane flight, each bag will cost you extra. The reason for the extra charge is the weight, the use of more space, and the use of more fuel.

Likewise, you are using up precious fuel and occupying precious space in your life with excess baggage! You have already carried and paid for it too long. There is a high probability that you continue to attract other people with a lot of baggage. Let God remove the junk and the residue. Trash – old hurt - must be removed, one thing at a time. It is a process to be willingly worked through with God the Holy Spirit as your Help.

What excess baggage do you carry on your shoulders, arms or hands that traps you in your journey through the narrow way? In the left column, indicate baggage you are unloading. On the right, indicate what you will pack for the journey. Remember! The things of God are spiritual, eternal AND light. (Matthew 11:30) You will need those for the long journey home. Please list below! TAKE YOUR TIME! THINK ABOUT WHAT YOU HOARD! REMOVE THE JUNK! DELETE IT!

REMOVE!   ETERNAL KEEPSAKES!

_____   _____

_____   _____

_____   _____

_____   _____

_____   _____

_____   _____

_____   _____

_____   _____

_____   _____

_____   _____

_____   _____

1.16 – CHURCH HURT!

Isaiah 1:18 – "Come now, and let us reason together, says the Lord: though your sins be as scarlet, they shall be as white as snow; though they be red like crimson, they shall be as wool.

Isaiah 53:6 – "All we like sheep have gone astray; we have turned every one to his own way; and the Lord hath laid on him the iniquity of us all."

Zechariah 13:7 – "...smite the shepherd, and the sheep shall be scattered:"

John 10:11 - "I am the Good Shepherd: the Good Shepherd gives his life for the sheep."

If you are a Christian, there is a very high probability that Church Hurt is somewhere in that pile of rubble inside of you, like the image on the previous page. Whether you are an Under-shepherd (Pastor) or one of the sheep, it seems almost inevitable that Church Hurt will visit you during the course of your Christian journey. That is a strange choice of words from God the Holy Spirit – "**Church Hurt will visit you.**" When I asked God for clarification, God said, "Visit means it doesn't HAVE to remain." I like that! The following brief story is injected here for your thoughts! DESIRE TO LAUGH AGAIN WITH GOD WHO LOVES YOU!

I was on my way to get my morning coffee at my friendly neighborhood coffee shop. As I drove, I registered my very vocal, passionate complaint about something for which I received the penalty. I said, "But I did NOTHING WRONG!" I repeated that a several times, as if God didn't hear me. Finally, God said, "Jesus didn't either." It was the way I heard God say it. I said a real hush-your-mouth kind of OOOPS! "Well, okay then. Thank You, God!" I laughed myself to tears. Jesus was innocent of ALL charges against Him. Sometimes, so are we. Based on I Peter 2:18, I like to think God gives us extra credit for those times.

Church Hurt has been a part of the Church since the beginning. There is nothing new there. In a way, I have grown to believe we should expect Church Hurt. Jesus – the Good Shepherd – was the first one to experience it in a major way, from the start, through betrayal of Judas, the denial of Peter, and on the cross. The Shepherd was smitten (hit, stuck, beaten) just as Zechariah 13:7 prophesied. Jesus was not guilty. Nevertheless, He was crucified. Jesus chose the very disciples who would inflict the hurt upon Him. He experienced the abandonment of His disciples, too. Yet, He never railed against anyone. When He said, "Father forgive them for they know not what they do", that included the soldiers and saints – the ones who were against Him, the ones who said they were for Him, but disappeared on him, you and me!

The Church was formed with wounded people, who suffered from Church Hurt. Imagine the hurt of the followers who were in the Upper Room waiting for the coming of God the Holy Spirit. They waited in grief. Church Hurt continued throughout the ministry of Paul, the first century Church, right through to today.

The lamentations detailed in 2 Timothy 4:9-16 about Paul's Church Hurt are heartbreaking. However, the hurt didn't immobilize him, as it often does us. Paul's testimony in 2 Timothy 4:17-18 is his praise that encourages us to embrace the "notwithstanding" perspective on Church Hurt or any other hurt. It offers us a key to know how we ascend beyond mere survival to be victorious; and advance the ministry of Jesus Christ beyond the hurt and in spite of it.

It is written:

2 Timothy 4:17-18 – "*Notwithstanding* the Lord stood with me, and strengthened me; that by me the preaching might be fully known, and that all the Gentiles might hear: and I was delivered out of the mouth of the lion. And the Lord shall deliver me from every evil work, and will preserve me unto his heavenly kingdom: to whom be glory forever and ever. Amen!"

Hear the resolve in Paul's voice to keep going forward for Christ. Church Hurt taught him that the Good Shepherd stands with us; and strengthens us. His preaching and ministry expanded. He says God delivered him from THAT hurt and other past hurt. Therefore, he was confident in the Lord that God would deliver him from the current and the future hurt. Paul celebrated not only the deliverance, but also God's preservation of God. He knew and believed that GOD already healed the spiritual wounds and broken places of His sheep. By prayer and faith, we work with God the Holy Spirit to see the manifestation of an accomplished fact, as well. DECIDE TO LET THE HURT GO!

Describe any Church Hurt, or disappointment with Church people that you experienced in your personal faith journey!

_____

_____

_____

_____

_____

_____

_____

_____

How was your worship of or service to God altered as a result of the Church Hurt or any hurt that you received?

_____

_____

_____

_____

_____

_____

_____

To this point, how have you addressed the wounds you received while serving?

_____

_____

_____

_____

Isaiah 1:18 gives God's response to us, and our sin that grieves God.   In what ways do you see this scripture as a model for how Christians should come together to reason and resolve Church Hurt or any hurt?

_____

_____

_____

_____

_____

_____

The prophecy in Isaiah 53:6-8 declares what Jesus accomplished for us through the hurt and pain He received on our behalf. How does this scripture apply to you and the Church Hurt you experienced?

_____

_____

_____

_____

_____

_____

_____

_____

Please read Matthew 27:45. It records that darkness covered the earth as Jesus hang on the cross. After years of wondering what that phenomenon of the creation meant, God the Holy Spirit revealed to the writer the following revelation concerning that darkness. The details are to be written in another book. Smile! But, consider this.

God said: *"I do some of my best work in the darkness of unknowing. In the crucifixion darkness, your sin, and the sin of the whole world, throughout all ages, was downloaded onto my Son. My blessings through Him were uploaded to you and all generations."*

Glory! Hallelujah! I didn't know whether to jump up in praise; bow down in worship; or curl up in the fetal position called prayer. So, I did all three! Both the creation story in Genesis 1- 2 and the salvation story of the re-creation that begins with Calvary in the Gospels prove that God does God's best work in the dark. Don't let the darkness frighten you. IT IS "ALL GOOD"!

What are the areas of darkness or uncertainty that resulted in your life as a result of Church Hurt or any hurt?

_____

_____

_____

_____

_____

_____

_____

Based on Romans 8:28 and where you are now in your walk with the Lord, reflect on that period of darkness that occurred following your Church Hurt or any hurt. Describe how you now see that God was at work, even in the darkness or waiting?

_____

_____

_____

_____

_____

_____

What did you learn about yourself through Church Hurt or any hurt?

_____

_____

_____

_____

What did you learn about God and your relationship to God as a result of your hurt?

_____

_____

_____

_____

Write a brief commentary about the benefit of the darkness of re-creation and Calvary as a way to heal your hurt. Hint: See the quote above.

_____

_____

_____

_____

_____

1.17 – GENERATIONAL BLESSINGS? GENERATIONAL CURSES?

Deuteronomy 28:2 – "And all these blessings shall come on you, and overtake you, if you shall hearken unto the voice of the Lord your God."

Nehemiah 13:2 – "...howbeit our God turned the curse into a blessing."

Galatians 3:13-14 – "Christ has redeemed us from the curse of the law, being made a curse for us: for it is written, cursed is every one that hangs on a tree: That the blessing of Abraham might come on the Gentiles through Jesus Christ; that we might receive the promise of the Spirit through faith."

Please read the entirety of Deuteronomy 28. Jesus took the penalty for the generational curses of the Law. Quickly examine your life and family history. There may be some generational curses over which you must take authority and work with God the Holy Spirit to declare Christ's blood and victory over them.

If you ask, God the Holy Spirit will show you where the generational curses are manifesting in your life. The repetitive pattern of negative behavior or crisis, in more than one generation or across a single generation, is an example that a generational curse is manifesting. Premature death across generational lines is another example. Compare Deuteronomy 28 to your family line or your life. See God's revelations. Then, write the blessings, and possible curses that could be in the trash pile. Declare that all the curses are broken and destroyed in the Name of Jesus.

Blessings   Curses

_____   _____

_____   _____

_____   _____

_____   _____

_____   _____

_____   _____

_____   _____

_____   _____

It is written:

Galatians 4:4-5 – "But when the fullness of the time was come, God sent forth his Son, made of a woman, made under the law, to redeem them that were under the law, that we might receive the adoption of sons."

Jesus redeemed us or purchased us back from the curse of all the law. Nothing and no one else could do it. Through the grace of Christ, and His accomplished work on the cross, we are now the adopted sons and daughters of God. Generational curses are broken. Therefore, they have no effect when we know, believe in, and declare the power of God over every condition of our natural and spiritual line and lineage.

Please write below, some blessings/benefits of your adoption as heirs/heiresses of God through the salvation work of Jesus Christ!

Blessings/Benefits

_____   _____

_____   _____

_____   _____

_____   _____

_____   _____

_____   _____

_____   _____

_____   _____

Please read Psalm 103, verbally. Then, verbally repeat the following simple prayer!

Most Holy God – Our Heavenly Father!

Thank You for every generational curse that is broken through Jesus Christ. Thank You for every blessing available and received through your grace and my obedience. I am Your child because of Your Son, and our Savior! I am free of all curses! I am abundantly blessed!

In the Name of Jesus!
Amen!

1.18 – PURGE!

Jeremiah15: 18-20 – "Why is my pain perpetual, and my wound incurable, which refuses to be healed? Wilt thou be altogether unto me as a liar, and as waters that fail? Therefore thus saith the Lord, if thou return, then will I bring thee again, and thou shalt stand before me: and **if thou take forth the precious from the vile, thou shalt be as my mouth**: let them return unto thee; but return not thou unto them. And I will make thee unto this people a fenced brazen wall: and they shall fight against thee, but they shall not prevail against thee: for I am with thee to save thee and to deliver thee, saith the Lord."

Based on Jeremiah 15:18-20, we are responsible to purge our spirit, souls, minds, bodies, and lives so that we may be healed. There is a direct relationship, according to this text, between the hurt we feel and the things we need to remove from our lives. Purging is getting rid of everything that does not glorify God. Purging is obedience to the Word of God. Hoarding is not! Jesus did His Work! The rest is on us!

If we take the precious things (things and people that add to our lives) from the vile (toxic people and corruptible things that diminish the qualify of life) God makes some promises that apply to our healing, deliverance, recovery, and victory.

1. God promises that the power of our voice will carry the power of the voice of God. With God's voice, God created everything that exists. Imagine that! We can re-create our circumstances with our voice when we are purged, delivered and recovered!

2. We will speak with power like God speaks; change our circumstances; and help God change the conditions of others! Our blessings wait for us to speak to see them.

3. God promises us that if we purge ourselves and return unto God, God will make us a fenced, brazen wall, like we discussed earlier!

4. God promises that our enemies will fight against us, but will not win!

5. God promises that God will be with us to save us!

6. God promises to deliver us!

7. The result is a heart, soul, mind and body that are free to love God!

Colossians 1:9-11 – "For this cause we also, since the day we heard it, do not cease to pray for you, and to desire that ye might be filled with the knowledge of his will in all wisdom and spiritual understanding; That ye might walk worthy of the Lord unto all pleasing, being fruitful in every good work, and increasing in the knowledge of God; Strengthened with all might, according to his glorious power, unto all patience and longsuffering with joyfulness;"

It is written:

Matthew 9:16-17 – "No man putteth a piece of new cloth unto an old garment, for that which is put in to fill it up taketh from the garment, and the rent (hole) is made worse. Neither do men put new wine into old bottles: else the bottles break, and the wine runneth out, and the bottles perish: but they put new wine into new bottles, and both are preserved."

This scripture, like all the Holy Bible, gives us critical revelation knowledge. GOD WILL NOT ADD new blessings to old stuff. It's not that God said no to you or your prayers. God's Word, precepts and doctrine stand. Old spiritual or emotional junk occupies the space. God will not add new to old. That is the Law of God.

 Please write Matthew 7:7-8.

_____

_____

_____

_____

_____

Please write your God-inspired thoughts on Matthew 7:7-8 below.

_____

_____

_____

_____

How do you apply Matthew 7:7-8 to the need to heal your hurt?

_____

_____

_____

_____

What are the actions that Matthew 7:7-8 require you to take?

_____

_____

_____

_____

Please write your God-inspired thoughts on Philippians 4:19 regarding your healing.

_____

_____

_____

_____

God cannot lie. God said it. That settles it, whether we believe it of not. God promised in God's word to give us blessings. God operates according to God's Word. God desires to bless us in all areas. However, God blesses us according to our obedience to the Word of God. Never permit the enemy to convince you to believe that God desires anything less than the best for the sons and daughters of God! That includes you!

We are obligated to purge ourselves through the power of God the Holy Spirit who lives in us. God the Holy Spirit will occupy and perfect what we submit and permit, daily.

Usually, what God desires to add to us is the exact opposite of what currently exists. For example, if you grieve, God desires to give you the oil of gladness.

Is the new wine of God the Holy Spirit leaking out of you? Do you have holes in your spiritual clothes? Just asking!

What new clothing of righteousness or new condition or blessing in character do you desire God to add to your life? Think big thoughts. Write them below! Obey God! Pray! Believe!

_____

_____

_____

_____

Please write your God-inspired thoughts about Psalm 37:4.

_____

_____

_____

_____

_____

Describe your delight toward God!

_____

_____

_____

_____

_____

What areas of your "delight in God" need improvement in your life?

_____

_____

_____

_____

_____

What desire(s) do you pray for God to fulfill for you?

_____

_____

_____

_____

_____

What will you surrender to God for purging/removal to make room for your desires to be fulfilled?

_____

_____

_____

_____

Please write your God-inspired thoughts about Luke 12:32.

_____

_____

_____

_____

What are the spiritual and natural needs that you will believe God to receive?

_____

_____

_____

_____

Describe what you believe are the unlimited riches of God that God desires to transfer to you?

_____

_____

_____

_____

Please describe who or what is standing between you and what God promises?

_____

_____

_____

_____

_____

What hinders you from purging the trash from your life – past and present?

_____

_____

_____

_____

_____

How do you imagine your life could be more Christ-Like and blessed if you permit God the Holy Spirit to purge you of junk?

_____

_____

_____

_____

Some people won't let go of the hurt/past because they fear the results. Some fear they will have nothing left. Others fear the new person they will become. Some fear the unknown. Fear is not of God! Have faith in God!

It is written:

2 Timothy 1:7 – "For God hath not given us the spirit of fear; but of power, and of love, and of a sound mind."

Please describe your fears or hesitation to work with God the Holy Spirit through the purging of the past, trash, people, or pain from your life.

_____

_____

_____

_____

_____

_____

Even negative experiences and people can teach us something. What beneficial lessons have you learned from the experiences and people that you now purge or let go?

_____

_____

_____

_____

_____

_____

_____

_____

What would be the worse thing that could happen to you if you expressed your hurt and let it all go?

_____

_____

_____

_____

_____

_____

1.19 – ROAD CALLED DELIVERANCE!

Deliverance and healing are two steps in the process of spiritual recovery from whatever is not God's will for our lives. We must permit God the Holy Spirit to deliver us from the past, however simple or complicated it is. Healing is always a past tense reality, according to Isaiah 53:5. Deliverance removes the residue and desire to go back to that from which God already healed us. When God delivers us, we journey freely with God the Holy Spirit on the road called Deliverance that leads to Victory in our present. We move forward in recovery. Recovery moves us away from the hurting place, and retrieves our magnificent story that Jesus wrote about us in the first place. Work with God to get to the Road Called Deliverance!

"I affirm the deliverance of Jesus Christ in my life from all faulty spiritual, intellectual, emotional and personality residue. I walk in the Spirit of Holiness, wholeness, and authority through the power of God the Holy Spirit."

In the Name of Jesus!
Amen!

Please rewrite this affirmation below. Sign and date it as your commitment to spiritual, intellectual, and emotional health!

_____

_____

_____

_____

Deliverance is a blessing of salvation. Jesus not only delivered us FROM the snares, tricks, and traps of the enemy, but God the Holy Spirit delivers us TO God for perfecting. We must believe that as we clear the ruble. In the spaces below, please indicate the things **from which** God has delivered you on the left. On the right, indicate the holy, spiritual blessings **to which** God the Holy Sprit now brings you.

DELIVERED FROM: **SAVED TO:**

_____   _____

_____   _____

_____   _____

_____   _____

_____   _____

_____   _____

_____   _____

_____   _____

_____   _____

_____   _____

_____   _____

_____   _____

_____   _____

_____   _____

_____   _____

_____   _____

1.20 – THE SPIRITUAL DWELLING PLACE!

Imagine these images as your new, personal spiritual dwelling place. What is the name that you give to your new spiritual home?

Name:

_____

These are the words that describe how I feel when I live in the spiritual place called Peace!

1. _____

2. _____

3. _____

4. _____

5. _____

6. _____

7. _____

8. _____

1.21 – SET FREE! LIVE FREELY!

John 8:36 – "If the Son therefore shall make you free, ye shall be free indeed."

Jesus Christ set us free to live in the authority of the sons and daughters of God. To live in that freedom requires the work of God the Holy Spirit and the believer.

Compared to your past, write a brief commentary that describes how your freedom in Christ looks or should look, or will look based on John 8:36.

_____

_____

_____

_____

All Yoked-Up!

I Kings 19:19 – "So he departed thence, and found Elisha the son of Shaphat, who was plowing with twelve yoke of oxen before him, and he with the twelfth: and Elijah passed by him, and cast his mantle upon him."

The image of Elisha plowing with animals is great with many powerful interpretations. One interpretation requires the question to be answered whether people should really be joked with animals? NO! Is there more? Yes! When Elijah passed the prophetic mantel to Elisha it indicated that Elisha was called from the old life to greater works. He prayed that God double the miracles that God worked through Elijah. God did just that. Jesus Christ set you free, breaks the yoke, and anoints you for greater works that are unimaginable. The anointing is the present working power of God that is "smeared" on us. We celebrate the power of God in us and on us. We embrace the God-Power that the anointing IS...not the "Buzz Word" version! Restore the rightful standing of "the anointing" in your spirit and soul. The anointing is God guaranteed power that God backs up with God's Word.

Identify any area of your life where you are yoked up with oxen of unbelief, the past or anything that is keeping you in the rut of your old life.

_____

_____

_____

_____

_____

_____

Isaiah 10:27 – "And it shall come to pass in that day, that his burden shall be taken away from off thy shoulder, and his yoke from off thy neck, and the yoke shall be destroyed because of the anointing."

According to Isaiah 10:27 and Isaiah 14:25, God breaks oppressive spirits in our lives, and destroys yokes. Burdens depart. Name the burdens God lifted for you in the past, and the burdens or oppressive spirits you believe God will lift now.

Past Burdens Lifted!   **Imagine Present Burdens Lifted!**

_____   _____

_____   _____

_____   _____

_____   _____

Nahum 1:13 – "For now will I break his yoke from off thee, and will burst thy bonds in asunder." (God removes the shackles, the chains that bind us.)

What does the promise in Nahum 1:13 mean to you concerning your present life?

_____

_____

_____

Matthew 11:29-30 – "Take my yoke upon you, and learn of me; for I am meek and lowly in heart: and ye shall find rest unto your souls. For my yoke is easy, and my burden is light."

Describe the difference in being yoked up with Christ, and yoked up with hurt!

_____

_____

_____

_____

God commands us!

Galatians 5:1 – "Stand fast therefore in the liberty wherewith Christ hath made us free, and be not entangled again with the yoke of bondage."

1.22 – AGAPE! CHRIST-LOVE!

GOD REQUIRES OUR
"WHOLE" LOVE –
HEART, SOUL, MIND!

Agape is the Greek word for love that only refers to the love that Jesus demonstrated on the cross AND yet demonstrates toward us, every day.   It is the Godly, sacrificial love of Christ that gives us what we need. We needed and yet need Jesus!

Define Agape (Christ-Love) in your own words based on John 3:16 and I Corinthians 13.

_____

_____

_____

_____

_____

_____

_____

_____

_____

_____

SECTION 2.0

HEART RENOVATION?
OR
TRANSPLANT?

2.1 – LOVE GOD WITH YOUR WHOLE HEART!
IT IS NOT OPTIONAL! ALL!

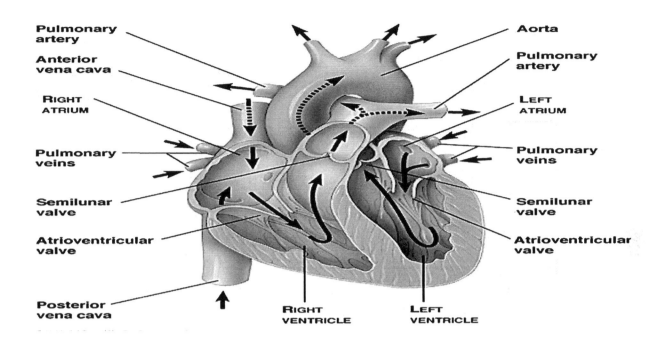

The physical heart, and all the parts connected to it, is the power center for an intricate, super highway system running through the human body. If the heart stops working, the blood, nutrients and the oxygen it transports to every part of us no longer flows correctly. Death is certain. A healthy heart is critical to physical life. The condition of the heart is also important for a healthy spiritual life.

While the physical heart is an incredible machine, the spiritual heart is even more powerful. For a quick fun review see: **36 Interesting Facts About The Human Heart** @http://facts.randomhistory.com/human-heart-facts.html. Compare them to the spiritual heart of your inner person.

Essentially in Matthew 22:37-40, Jesus commands us to love God with everything that gives life, sustains life, and makes abundant life and living possible. In other words, Jesus says, love God with life and our very lives. Connect your life to the Blood supply of Jesus that never loses its power. It is the Source for abundant life.

Just as a healthy blood supply is essential to the life of the physical body, the Blood of Jesus is infinitely more essential to the physical and spiritual body, soul and spirit. The Blood of Jesus is essential for the new, converted Christ-Life. The spiritual heart pumps life-giving elements through every part of the spiritual, inner person. There is power in the Blood!

Look again at the image of the human heart. Write your own commentary on the importance of both a healthy physical and spiritual heart to entirely love God, and live!

_____

_____

_____

_____

_____

_____

_____

_____

_____

_____

_____

How do you compare the need for healthy love for your spiritual body with the need for a healthy blood supply to your physical body?

_____

_____

_____

_____

_____

_____

_____

God commands us to love God with all of our hearts! How are you doing with that portion of the Commandment? Please describe below.

_____

_____

_____

_____

_____

_____

2.2 – HEART CONDITIONS!

How many mornings has God awaken you and you asked yourself, "What is the condition of my heart today?" If you are like most people, the answer is never. Yet, the condition of the heart impacts the rest of the body and thus our very lives. To be spiritually healthy requires that we examine the condition of our hearts on a regular basis – our physical and spiritual hearts.

The Holy Bible uses many descriptions for the condition of the heart that we should consider.

Psalm 109:22 – "For I am poor and needy, and my heart is wounded within me."

Describe below at least one occasion when your heart was wounded or broken.

_____

_____

_____

_____

_____

_____

_____

_____

Psalm 51:10 - "Create in me a clean heart, O God; and renew a right spirit within me."

How does a clean heart look and how does your heart compare?

_____

_____

_____

_____

_____

2 Timothy 2:22 - "Flee also youthful lusts: but follow righteousness, faith, charity, peace with them that call on the Lord out of a pure heart."

On a scale of 1-10 with 10 as the mark of a pure heart, please evaluate the following. Circle one.

I have run away from all youthful lusts to purify my heart.

1   2   3   4   5   6   7   8   9   10

I follow righteousness to purify my heart.

1   2   3   4   5   6   7   8   9   10

I follow faith out of a pure heart.

1   2   3   4   5   6   7   8   9   10

I follow charity (love) out of a pure heart.

1   2   3   4   5   6   7   8   9   10

I follow peace out of a pure heart.

1   2   3   4   5   6   7   8   9   10

I see evidence that I need to improve!

1   2   3   4   5   6   7   8   9   10

Hebrews 10:22 – "Let us draw near with a true heart in full assurance of faith having our hearts sprinkled from an evil conscience, and our bodies washed with pure water."

Write a brief commentary on what you believe a Godly conscience looks like in action .

_____

_____

_____

_____

_____

_____

_____

_____

_____

2.3 – HEART EXAMINATION!

On a scale of 1-10 (10 is the highest) rank your current or past heart condition. Think thoughtfully and prayerfully. Carefully circle one of the numbers on each line.

1. Stony Heart   1   2   3   4   5   6   7   8   9   10

2. Broken Heart   1   2   3   4   5   6   7   8   9   10

3. Fearful Heart   1   2   3   4   5   6   7   8   9   10

4. Lonely Heart   1   2   3   4   5   6   7   8   9   10

5. Doubtful Heart   1   2   3   4   5   6   7   8   9   10

6. Loving Heart   1   2   3   4   5   6   7   8   9   10

7. Lustful Heart   1   2   3   4   5   6   7   8   9   10

8. Angry Heart   1   2   3   4   5   6   7   8   9   10

9. Obedient Heart   1   2   3   4   5   6   7   8   9   10

10. Grieving Heart   1   2   3   4   5   6   7   8   9   10

11. Pure Heart   1   2   3   4   5   6   7   8   9   10

12. True Heart   1   2   3   4   5   6   7   8   9   10

13. Prayerful Heart   1   2   3   4   5   6   7   8   9   10

14. Humble Heart   1   2   3   4   5   6   7   8   9   10

15. Joyful Heart   1   2   3   4   5   6   7   8   9   10

16. Generous Heart   1   2   3   4   5   6   7   8   9   10

17. Strong Heart   1   2   3   4   5   6   7   8   9   10

18. Repentant Heart   1   2   3   4   5   6   7   8   9   10

19. Grateful Heart   1   2   3   4   5   6   7   8   9   10

20. Compassionate Heart   1   2   3   4   5   6   7   8   9   10

21. Passionate Heart   1   2   3   4   5   6   7   8   9   10

22. Faithful Heart   1   2   3   4   5   6   7   8   9   10

23. Courageous Heart   1   2   3   4   5   6   7   8   9   10

24. Contented Heart   1   2   3   4   5   6   7   8   9   10

25. Other Heart   1   2   3   4   5   6   7   8   9   10

The writer is so excited about God's revelation for the next exercise. Please follow the instructions below.

- Use a ruler and pencil to carefully draw a line to connect the numbers you circled from items 1-25. (You understand that many more conditions could be included.)

- When finished, turn the pages horizontally.

- What you should see is the rhythm of your heart over the years – a spiritual electro-cardiogram.

Scientists and medical professionals prove that there is a direct impact to the physical heart from our life experiences. For example, Broken Heart Syndrome is real. Emotions like stress, grief, fear, etc., are the cause. (See: http://video.msnbc.msn.com/nightly-news). On the other hand, evidence also shows that the condition of the physical heart and blood pressure can be improved when we live healthy physical lifestyles. Imagine what happens when we live healthy Godly lives. The physical person and spiritual person improve.

Many people never consider how negative people, emotions, and experiences can clog our spiritual veins and arteries, and ruin their overall health. In the same way that blockages or simply unhealthy blood flow occurs in the physical body, we can apply the principle to our spiritual body.

Continuous, constant, consistent change is necessary so that we love God with ALL of our heart – without arrhythmic (skipping) beats. God requires that we live in determination to give God control over the life center – the heart. Then we fully reap the harvest and reflect the lifestyle of the Christ-Life as we walk after the Spirit, according to Galatians 5. The Fruit of the Spirit is our reality.

Please read Galatians 5:16-26. What are the most immediate changes that are necessary in your life to increase your walk after the Spirit?

_____

_____

_____

What difference in your spiritual walk do you expect from these changes?

_____

_____

_____

2.4 – CHECK YOUR ROOTS!

Hebrews 12:14-16

"Follow peace with all men, and holiness, without which no man shall see the Lord: Looking diligently lest any man fail of the grace of God; lest any root of bitterness springing up trouble you, and thereby many be defiled; Lest there be any fornicator, or profane person, as Esau, who for one morsel of meat sold his birthright."

ROOT OF BITTERNESS!

The roots of a plant/tree are key to its survival. Roots anchor plants and trees; and absorb water, minerals, and nutrients that they need to live. On the surface of the seed is the initial root called the Radicle. In its early stages, it is undetectable with the naked eye. The taproot is the strong root that sinks deeply, and helps hold the plant/tree in place. Without evidence on the surface of the plant or tree, an elaborate root system forms and continues to grow.

We use the imagery of the root system on the previous page to apply to our hearts. Hebrews 12:14-16 addresses the act of repression, beginning with the word "lest". Repression is the conscious or unconscious act that is used to avoid addressing, examining and eliminating any or all painful ideas, memories, experiences, feelings, emotions or impulses. There is a direct connection between repression and the root of bitterness about which the scripture speaks. In other words, like the root system of a plant or tree grows below the ground undetected, the root of bitterness in us is most often undetected, also.

The root of bitterness cannot remain. It poisons or chokes our entire spiritual and physical systems. It hinders the flow of God's blessedness, and the interior work of God the Holy Spirit. According to Hebrews 12:14-16, the root of bitterness will spring up and "trouble" us. It will not leave on its own. We examine ourselves and pull it up in the spirit. More unhealthy roots may grow deeply and snarly, as they entwine with other roots like those in the image. They will be painful to pull up. Begin the excavation process of your heart through prayer! They must GO!

Write on the previous image your unhealthy roots. Then, describe below the first root of bitterness – the spiritual Radicle Root – that you remember to begin the process of pulling up unhealthy roots. God the Holy Spirit will reveal others over time. Let no bitterness take root. PRAY!

_____

_____

_____

_____

_____

_____

How has the root of bitterness sprung up in your life and caused trouble for you?

_____

_____

_____

_____

_____

Like anything else that is alive and grows, a root of bitterness and other unhealthy roots can only grow in optimum or favorable conditions. Please describe below the conditions like anger, rage, stress, depression, jealousy, disappointment, grief, etc. that you permitted in your life that kept these roots alive and helped to increase their size and volume.

_____

_____

_____

_____

On a scale of 1 to 10 (10 is the highest), how much has each of the following contributed to the development of the root system of bitterness? Circle one number for each contributor.

2.5 – Root System Contributors Sample									
Deception	1	2	3	4	5	6	7	8	9	10
Anger	1	2	3	4	5	6	7	8	9	10
Resentment	1	2	3	4	5	6	7	8	9	10
Denial	1	2	3	4	5	6	7	8	9	10
Disappointment	1	2	3	4	5	6	7	8	9	10
Abandonment	1	2	3	4	5	6	7	8	9	10
Betrayal	1	2	3	4	5	6	7	8	9	10
Loss of Loved One	1	2	3	4	5	6	7	8	9	10
Loss of Dream(s)	1	2	3	4	5	6	7	8	9	10
Mistakes	1	2	3	4	5	6	7	8	9	10
Neglect	1	2	3	4	5	6	7	8	9	10
Pretense	1	2	3	4	5	6	7	8	9	10

Just as old sin dis-eases must be mortified (killed off) because they will not leave on their own, the root of bitterness and other unhealthy roots must be pulled up. When the roots are gone, spiritual veins and arteries are opened to new life.

Indicated below is a brief prayer. Please repeat the prayer aloud. As you write the roots that are imbedded in your heart that cannot remain, repeat the prayer over each one, in faith. Even if you don't think you have any roots to be pulled up, chances are much more likely that you do. Generally, just living and life make it so. Don't let repression hold you hostage. Deliverance, recovery, restoration and freedom are a part of God's plan for your life and your goals!

Prayer: Holy and Righteous God: By the power of God the Holy Spirit, I pull up the root of bitterness and all unhealthy roots in my life that are attached to it.

In the Name of Jesus!
Amen!"

ROOT OF BITTERNESS AND UNHEALTHY ROOTS REMOVED!

_____ _____

_____ _____

_____ _____

_____ _____

_____ _____

_____ _____

_____ _____

_____ _____

_____ _____

2.6 - Affairs of the Heart – Forgiveness!

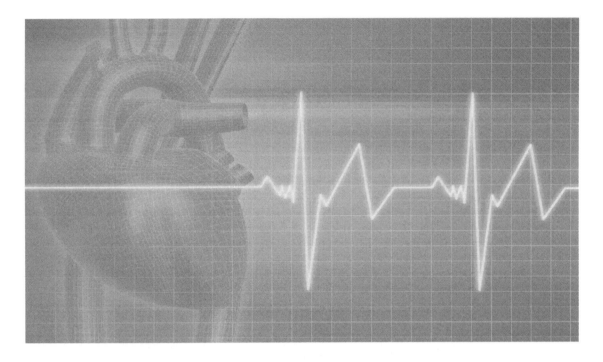

Failure or refusal to forgive "YOU" and/or forgive others is the enemy's attack on your heart. A heart attack is in progress. That heart attack causes spiritual, emotional and indirectly physical death! Unwillingness to forgive becomes a stronghold that the enemy sets up to devour you from the inside out.

Are you flat lining, minute by minute because of unforgiveness or other issues and you don't know it?

Yes _____ No _____ Unsure _____

The irony is that the other person is most often not even aware of our hurt. If they are, they probably don't care. Yet, we continue to do great spiritual and/or emotional damage to ourselves through unforgiveness. So, what's the point of self-inflicted wounds? Below, please explain to God why you can't/won't forgive yourself or someone else!

_____

_____

_____

_____

IS NEW LIFE FLOWING TO YOU, AND FROM YOU TO OTHERS THE WAY JESUS INTENDED AND REQUIRES? Please check one: Yes _____ No _____ Not Sure _____

It is written:

Matthew 6:12 – "And forgive us our debts, as we forgive our debtors."

The Living Translation (2007) says: "and forgive us our sins, as we have forgiven those who sin against us."

Matthew 18:21-23 – "Then came Peter to him, and said, Lord, how oft shall my brother sin against me, and I forgive him? Till seven times? Jesus saith unto him, I say not unto thee, until seven times: but, until seventy times seven."

Colossians 3:13 – "Forbearing one another, and forgiving one another, if any man have a quarrel against any: even as Christ forgave you, so also do ye."

God requires us to forgive. Forgiveness is such an important Christian doctrine (teaching of Jesus). We tend to put limits on the extent to which we will go to forgive another. Yet, forgiveness is for our benefit. Forgiveness of our sin runs parallel to our forgiveness of others. Besides! Jesus forgave us! That's an undeniable incentive. What if He refused? How much would we still owe God? HMMM! Jesus was the only acceptable sacrifice for our forgiveness. He died to reconcile us to God (bring us to right fellowship with God)!

In Matthew 18:21-23, Jesus teaches us that we are to forgive 490 times for each offense perpetrated. In other words, keep going until you get there – the place called forgiveness. Forgiveness is unlimited. In a sense, Jesus dares us to try to keep count of each time we forgive someone for each offense. Even when we do try to keep count, we forget. The irony is we recognize the futility of attempting to keep a record. We basically have to let it go because of the irrationality of the exercise.

Forgiveness will be dealt with more extensively in Seminar II. However, there is no time like the present to take a quick look at the people we need to forgive, as well as, those from whom we should seek forgiveness, including ourselves! Hopefully, by the time you reach Seminar II, you will be already healed from unforgiveness!

People I forgive!   People who I desire to forgive me!

_____   _____

_____   _____

_____   _____

_____   _____

How do you continue to hurt yourself because you have not forgiven yourself?

_____

_____

_____

_____

_____

In many ways, when we don't forgive ourselves, we have more difficulty forgiving others. We have a tendency to transfer our guilt to them.

List below every negative thought that you have or negative comment about yourself that either you and/or the enemy (NOT GOD) continue to bring up about your past to condemn and hurt you.

_____   _____

_____   _____

_____   _____

_____   _____

_____   _____

_____   _____

_____   _____

_____   _____

The Name of Jesus rebukes (stops) and smashes the negative, unhealthy, unholy record, eight track, and the cd that keep playing in your head.

Remember! It is written:

I John 1:9 – "If we confess our sins, he (God) is faithful and just to forgive us our sins, and to cleanse us from all unrighteousness."

Ask our loving God to forgive you! Eloquence is not required, just faith that God keeps the promise of I John 1:9.   Below, please write your own personal note to God to ask God's forgiveness! Include some of the things you were hoping God didn't see or forgot. God has been waiting on you to do just that. Smile! Then thank God for the forgiveness God gives.

_____

_____

_____

_____

_____

_____

_____

If you confessed your sin, God forgives you. God the Holy Spirit does not authorize you to continue in self-condemnation, according to scripture.

It is written:

Proverbs 16:7 – "When a man's ways please the Lord, he maketh even his enemies to be at peace with him."

Romans 8:1 – "There is therefore NOW no condemnation to them who are in Christ Jesus, who walk not after the flesh, but after the Spirit."

Unforgiveness is a form of condemnation. A condemned criminal is placed in prison. Often, we assign others and ourselves to prison through unforgiveness. We have no authority to condemn anyone, including ourselves. Forgiveness is our declaration that the offense or hurt has no power over us. God is on the throne.

According to the scriptures, God declares you are fit and valued because of Christ. God does not condemn you. No one else has the authority to do so, including you. The act of faith to receive forgiveness that we must take is to ask God to forgive us. According to the above scriptures, which are directed to Christians, not the world, God grants forgiveness to us, and declares there is no condemnation, no further penalty, for the sons and daughters of God.

Since God forgives you, forgive yourself and others so that you may love the Lord your God, the Forgiver, with all your heart, soul, and mind; love yourself, and love others. Christ has set you free. Walk in forgiveness. Enjoy the "SONshine".

2.7 – TRANSPLANT? A NEW HEART?

Ezekiel 11:19 – "And I will give them one heart, and I will put a new spirit within you; and I will take the stony heart out of their flesh, and will give them an heart of flesh:"

Ezekiel 18:31 – "Cast away from you all your transgressions, whereby ye have transgressed; and make you a new heart and a new spirit: for why will ye die, O house of Israel?"

Ezekiel 36:26 – "A new heart also will I give you, and a new spirit will I put within you: and I will take away the stony heart out of your flesh, and I will give you an heart of flesh."

At the beginning of Section 2.0, the question is posed: Heart Renovation or Transplant? The question focuses our attention on the range of truth in the Holy Bible concerning the condition of the heart. At a minimum, each of us needs to pray to God for a renovation, a change, in our heart. That requires us to work with God the Holy Spirit for the renovation to occur, daily.

The three passages above teach us that God will give us a new heart – a heart transplant. As we examine the condition of our hearts, we may see the need for a totally new heart. The spiritual heart transplant requires us to improve the care of the new spiritual heart, as we work out our own salvation (like digging for gold in a gold mine) with fear and trembling (Philippians 2:12) or the new heart will end up like the old one.   A new spiritual heart can improve your physical heart and total life.

If your heart is broken, it doesn't work correctly.   How will a spiritual heart transplant help? In other words, how would a brand new heart work better than the one you currently have?

_____

_____

_____

_____

_____

_____

_____

_____

_____

_____

_____

God can do anything but fail – including spiritual Cardiology!

How has your need to give or receive love in the past caused you heart trouble?

_____

_____

_____

_____

_____

_____

How does the way you communicate love to others compare to I Corinthians 13?

_____

_____

_____

_____

_____

_____

_____

What characteristics do you see about how you give or receive love need to be changed?

_____

_____

_____

_____

_____

Based on I Corinthians 13, how has the Agape Love of Christ for you given you hope and faith for the kind of love you give and need to receive?

_____

_____

_____

_____

_____

Based on Ezekiel 18:31, briefly list your past transgressions that caused damage to your heart.

_____

_____

_____

_____

_____

_____

According to Ezekiel 11:19, identify the blockages - stony places or hard-hearted portions of your heart that must be revealed to determine if the new heart is necessary.   Please describe honestly!

_____

_____

_____

_____

_____

_____

_____

Based on the First and Great Commandment, what will you do differently to ensure that you love God with all your heart, first?

_____

_____

_____

_____

_____

_____

_____

_____

Seek God's revelation. Then, please answer the following question! How will you creatively love yourself in a way that is pleasing to God as you go forward?

_____

_____

_____

_____

_____

_____

_____

Describe specific ways you will love others in a healthy, Godly way going forward?

_____

_____

_____

_____

_____

_____

_____

_____

_____

What will you do differently to keep your renovated or new heart love-healthy?

_____

_____

_____

_____

_____

_____

_____

_____

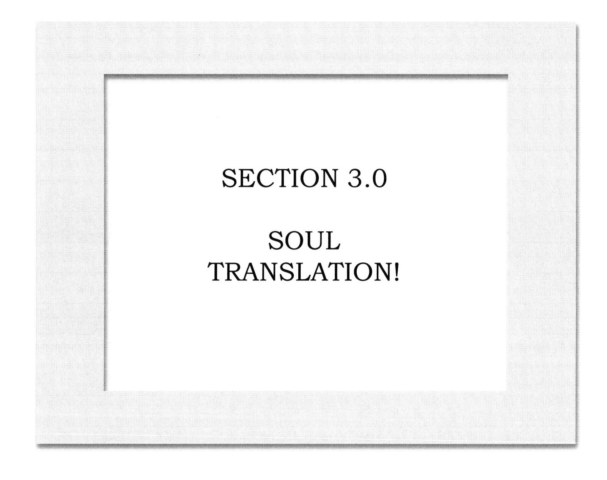

SECTION 3.0

SOUL
TRANSLATION!

3.1 – LOVE GOD WITH ALL OF YOUR SOUL!

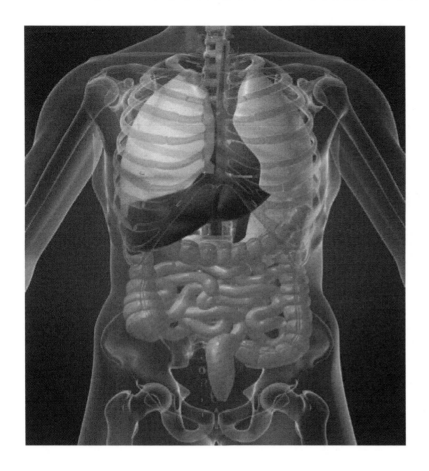

Spiritual Dwarfism?

The word soul is mentioned 432 times in the King James Version of the Holy Bible. The soul is extremely important, though relative to other things in life, it is dangerously disregarded.

The spiritual "you" that lives inside will never die. Honestly describe that person below.

_____

_____

_____

_____

_____

_____

_____

_____

If a picture is worth a thousand words, what are the single words that describe the picture of your inner person?

Positive Words: About You!   Words to Describe Need for Change!

_____   _____

_____   _____

_____   _____

_____   _____

_____   _____

_____   _____

_____   _____

_____   _____

The inner or spiritual person should be as large or larger than the physical person, and not a spiritual dwarf. Describe the ways that YOU work with God the Holy Spirit to grow the spiritual you from the inside out.

_____

_____

_____

_____

_____

What is your greatest challenge to working with God the Holy Spirit to grow your spiritual person?

_____

_____

_____

_____

_____

_____

_____

_____

Describe your perception of the quality of your spiritual being.

_____

_____

_____

_____

_____

_____

_____

The soul is the most important component of a person because the soul and spirit are the only parts of which we are that are eternal. Therefore, it is vital to remain conscientious about the care of our souls. Soul care facilitates the reproduction of the Fruit of the Spirit – the spiritual qualities that God the Holy Spirit gives us. When is the last time you checked the condition of your soul?

Please write new ways you believe you can work with God the Holy Spirit to care for your soul more effectively.

_____

_____

_____

_____

_____

_____

_____

Briefly describe the value you place on your soul?

_____

_____

_____

_____

_____

_____

3.2 – FROM CREATION TO RE-CREATION!

God is the Trinity. God is God in Three Persons – God the Father, God the Son, God the Holy Spirit. The True God is the Three-in-One God who created us in a tri-unity of body, soul, and spirit! It is written:

Genesis 2:7 – "And the Lord God formed man of the dust of the ground, and breathed into his nostrils the breath of life; and man became a living soul."

Consider the breath that is in your natural body. God the Holy Spirit re-creates us in tri-unity of spirit, soul and body! Spirit and soul are the indestructible, primary essence of who we are. It is written:

1 Thessalonians 5:23 – "And the very God of peace sanctify you wholly; and I pray God your whole spirit and soul and body be preserved blameless unto the coming of our Lord Jesus Christ."

According to I Thessalonians 5:23, God reorders our natural creation through the process of rebirth. Spirit and soul become primary. Disorder in the spirit and soul (the inner person) causes dysfunction in the entire life of a person both spiritually, mentally, and physically.

How will you work with God the Holy Spirit to give God total control over your spirit and soul?

_____

_____

_____

_____

_____

_____

_____

_____

_____

_____

_____

_____

_____

_____

In what ways will you sanctify yourself or set yourself apart in this season of your Christian journey?

_____

_____

_____

_____

_____

What are the unresolved issues that are associated with the unrest in your soul and spirit because of past experiences?

_____

_____

_____

_____

Based on 1 Thessalonians 5:23, God the Holy Spirit re-creates us to become spirit, soul and body; and sanctifies us (sets us apart from the world unto God). The goal is: "that your whole spirit and soul and body be preserved blameless unto the coming of our Lord Jesus Christ." Therefore, our blessed state of blamelessness requires that we release "blame" we hold over others or ourselves.

How have you either knowingly or unknowing cast blame on yourself or others?

_____

_____

_____

_____

Please name the specific blame, below! Confess it. Write a brief prayer to God to remove it and the spirit of blame that hinder you!

_____

_____

_____

_____

_____

3.3 – WHAT IS PSUCHE?

- The Greek word psuche or soul describes the immaterial, indestructible component of humans.

- We are the only creatures that God made that possess a soul. Animals are soulish. Generally, they take the character qualities of their owner, environment or experiences.

- No one knows conclusively where the soul is located because of the immaterial quality. However, we are confident that it is the essence of the inner person because of the way the Holy Bible speaks of it.

- Hebrews 4:12 tells us that the soul and spirit are so intrinsically connected together that only the Word of God can move between them or separate them.

- Our soul and spirit are immortal which means they will not die. They are the only part of us for which Jesus will return; or that will go to hell. Therefore, the soul and spirit should be our most important concern.

- God the Holy Spirit works with our spirit that seems to be housed in our soul. I suggest that like the skull is the cavity for the brain, and the brain is the cavity for the mind, the soul contains the spirit.

- The work of God the Holy Spirit through the soul and spirit is to transform us back to the spiritual image of God that was lost at the Fall of Humankind in the Garden of Eden.

- Our spirit never sleeps. Therefore, the spirit of humankind can receive constant messages from God, self, or satan (lower case on purpose). These messages include divine revelations, visions, dreams or nightmares.

- At all times, we need clear channels in our souls and spirits to send and receive communication from God the Holy Spirit, who is present with us.

- The religious and social/scientific/medical communities agree that the soul consists of the mind, the will, and the emotions.

- Imagination is also included in our model of the soul.

- The intense study of the soul dates back to antiquity and Galen, the Greek medical doctor (ca. 130-ca. 210 AD). The debate about the location of the soul continues till the present, and probably forever.

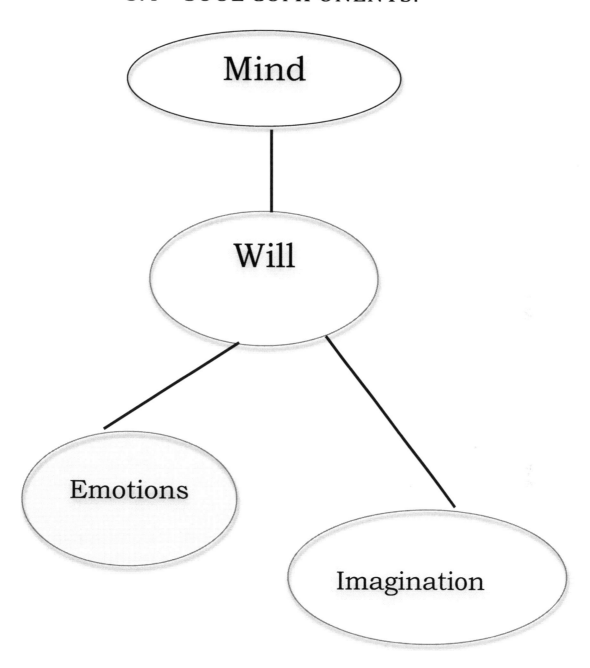

**Who or what controls
your will?
God? Self? Satan? Other?
Circle one!**

3.5 – WHERE ARE YOU?
WHERE IS YOUR SOUL?

1 Samuel 18:1 – "And it came to pass, when he had made an end of speaking unto Saul, that the soul of Jonathan was knit with the soul of David, and Jonathan loved him as his own soul."

Psalm 23:3 – "He restoreth my soul: He leadeth me in the paths of righteousness for his name's sake."

Matthew 10:28 – "And fear not them which kill the body, but are not able to kill the soul: but rather fear Him which is able to destroy both soul and body in hell."

Hebrews 4:12 – "For the word of God is quick, and powerful, and sharper than any two edged sword, piercing even to the dividing asunder of soul and spirit, and of the joints and marrow, and is a discerner of the thoughts and intents of the heart."

Based on I Samuel 18:1, we have evidence that our souls – the mind, the will, the emotions, and the imagination – can become attached to or united with the souls of other people. It is literally possible for two souls to become one, according to the scripture. Since that is true, we embrace the revelation that our souls or our essence can be scattered in many places with many people – both righteous people and unrighteous people.

If your soul is connected and therefore scattered among many people, it is impossible to completely obey God's command to LOVE GOD WITH ALL YOUR SOUL. This is especially true if our souls are attached to people, places and things that no longer bring Christian, spiritual value to our lives.

The question is posed above – where are you? If we are mentally, spiritually, or emotionally attached to someone or something, our minds, wills, emotions and imaginations are not at home with us. We are located where various portions of our souls are. Therefore, our souls are not available to us to love God with the totality required. Often, the relationship through which our souls became attached is not or was not mutually beneficial in the first place.

A symbiotic, mutually beneficial relationship is a healthy relationship. In a Christian symbiotic relationship, each person puts value on the other person's life and the relationship like Jesus places on that life and His relationship with us. A Christian symbiotic relationship is based on Agape – sacrificial, unconditional love. No one feels like he/she is disadvantaged. Symbiotic relationships can help prevent hurt, including Church Hurt. If symbiosis is not present in the relationship, it is a good indicator that Christ probably isn't either. It can still be a relationship, but did God ordain it; or does God approve of it?

Proverbs 4:23 – "Keep thy heart with all diligence; for out of it are the issues of life.

Proverbs 18:24 – "A man that hath friends must shew himself friendly: and there is a friend that sticketh closer than a brother.

SYMBIOTIC RELATIONSHIPS!

RELATIONSHIP BASE: MATTHEW 22:37-40
LOVE GOD! LOVE SELF! LOVE OTHERS!

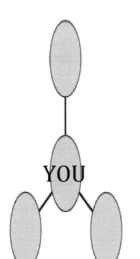

Characteristics of a Godly Symbiotic Relationship!

(Note: This diagram represents you and clusters of relationships! The clusters can be family, church, business relationships, neighbors, etc.!)

1) Christ's Agape (Unconditional / Sacrificial) Love is present.
2) GOD'S PRESENCE IN YOUR LIFE IS KNOWN AND RESPECTED!
3) Giving and receiving are balanced.
4) Everyone is and feels valued.
5) Benefits are mutual.

3.6 - HEALTHY PERSONAL RELATIONSHIPS

Giving  Receiving

Identify your key, healthy, symbiotic (mutually beneficial) relationships with specific people in your life (the relationships where giving and receiving are balanced). Honestly examine the above characteristics of the relationships before adding a name to the list.

_____   _____

_____   _____

_____   _____

_____   _____

_____   _____

3.7 - HEALTHY MINISTRY RELATIONSHIPS!

Giving ☰ Blessings of Discipleship

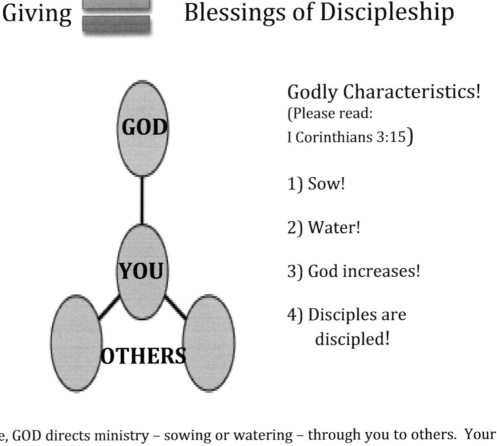

Godly Characteristics!
(Please read:
I Corinthians 3:15)

1) Sow!

2) Water!

3) God increases!

4) Disciples are
   discipled!

In this image, GOD directs ministry – sowing or watering – through you to others. Your soul (mind, will, emotions, imagination) may attach to the people or the ministry itself. God assigns you to either sow or water. God increases. Disciples are reproduced and edified (built up) for the Kingdom of God.

List the ministries/community service to which you are certain God assigned you. Beside each, place either an **"S"** for sower (one who plants/planted the seed)) or a **"W"** for waterer (one who nourishes/nourished what someone else planted).

_____   _____

_____   _____

_____   _____

_____   _____

_____   _____

What are the benefits to the Kingdom of God and specific blessings that you readily identify that your ministry relationships and/or community service bring to others AND you?

_____

_____

_____

_____

From the list of ministries or community service that you identified and others from the past, describe ministries that are or were healthy. Healthy ministry reflects Godly worship; operative Spiritual Gifts; fruitfulness, edification and spiritual growth of the members. In other words, God get the praise. Your service blesses others.

_____

_____

_____

_____

_____

Have you experienced ministry or community service in the past or present that you know was/is toxic to your spirit and soul? Please describe briefly.

_____

_____

_____

How will you modify or change your behavior to prevent that situation from reoccurring?

_____

_____

_____

_____

3.8 – UNHEALTHY RELATIONSHIPS!
SCATTERED SOUL!

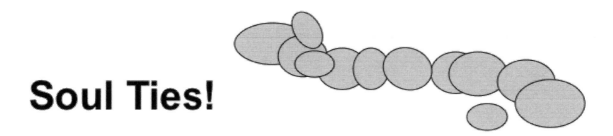

Soul Ties!

Based on 1 Samuel 18:1, it is critical that we observe to whom or to what our souls are connected. At a minimum, unhealthy soul ties can be draining; and at a maximum dangerous, specifically if the relationship is not God ordained. It is written:

I John 4:1-3 – "Beloved, believe not every spirit, but try the spirits whether they are of God: because many false prophets are gone out into the world. Hereby know ye the Spirit of God: Every spirit that confesses that Jesus Christ is come in the flesh is of God: and every spirit that confesses not that Jesus Christ is come in the flesh is not of God: and this is that spirit of antichrist, whereof ye have heard that it should come; and even now already is it in the world."

This scripture gives us a word of warning that is particularly important to our soul's health. We must test the spirit of the persons with whom we align ourselves to determine the spiritual identity. Many years ago, God the Holy Spirit taught me to ask the following question, in the spirit. "Are you the one who believes that Jesus is the Christ?" Trust God to reveal the answer. Usually, if you have to ask the question, chances are the spirit in that person is not one with whom you should connect, even on a casual basis. STOP! IT IS UNHEALTHY!

The illustration above gives us a visual example of how pieces of our soul can be scattered in many places, among many people. Our souls can attach to many things, experiences, and unresolved issues. So, to obey the command to love God with all our soul is difficult, if not impossible.

Below, please identify the unhealthy relationships in your current and past life based on the model. Pray for your soul to return to you from them. In other words, take your soul back.

_____   _____

_____   _____

_____   _____

Based on what God the Holy Spirit prompts you please use single words to describe why you are holding on to unhealthy relationships.

_____   _____

_____   _____

_____   _____

_____   _____

_____   _____

What hinders you from retrieving your soul – mind, will, emotions, imagination – from all the unhealthy relationships in your life, whether past or present?

_____

_____

_____

_____

In what way will your relationship with God benefit from retrieving your soul from unhealthy relationships, places, and memories?

_____

_____

_____

_____

What new thoughts will you think about the command to love God with all your soul to prevent attaching your soul to unhealthy relationships in the future?

_____

_____

_____

_____

_____

_____

3.9 – GRIEF AND SOUL TIES!

In 1969, Elizabeth Kübler-Ross presented a groundbreaking model for managing grief and grief counseling. Originally, it was based on the death and dying process with 500 participants in her study. She developed the theory that is commonly known as **The Five Stages of Grief**. Subsequently, others expanded upon her original model. However, the Kübler-Ross Model is our model of choice because it was the first one identified; and the one with which the writer is most familiar through effective and successful grief counseling over the years.

The Kübler-Ross Model for the five stages of grief is commonly known as the acronym **DABDA.** The five stages in her model are:

1) Denial; 2) Anger; 3) Bargaining; 4) Depression; and 5) Acceptance.

For further description of these five stages of grief, please visit the following website – www.http://grief.com/the-five-stages-of-grief/. You are encouraged to read carefully the general description of each stage to use now or in the future.

As Kübler-Ross later explained, the stages that were initially applied to death and dying can also be applied to other loss or catastrophic loss. The stages can take place over several years, and vary in order. Generally speaking, counseling professionals have research to support their premise that the recovery process for grief from death averages seven years. The Lord's report is that it can be shorter.

Identify below people who are deceased for whom you still grieve. Beside each name, write the number of years since they passed.

_____   _____

_____   _____

_____   _____

Identify below people who are alive for whom you still grieve the loss of the relationship. Include the number of years since the relationship ended.

_____   _____

_____   _____

_____   _____

_____   _____

Identify catastrophic events or losses about which you continue to have an emotional response. Write the number of years since it occurred beside it.

_____   _____

_____   _____

_____   _____

Good Grief and Soul Ties

Grief is an extremely complex condition that every human being will likely experience at some point along the journey. Grief counseling with a professional is recommended for those who find it difficult to begin or complete the recovery process. Christians are notorious for thinking they can recover without help. God works through professional counselors, too. There is no shame in seeking help!

Good grief is the deliberate, intentional, precise, progressive, process of moving forward in Christ to heal the broken places in our lives through the supernatural power of God the Holy Spirit. The Holy Comforter works in us and through others for us. We understand that we are processed through grief to greater encounter with God. We recognize that in the midst of our worse pain, in our darkness hour, the glory of God is yet available for us to see. Seek to see God!

As previously stated, mental health professionals report that the normal grief process can last seven years. That is the acceptable standard. However, the recovery process varies, like the Huber-Ross **Five Stages of Grief** model demonstrates. Based on pastoral counseling experience, the writer suggests that through Christ the process of recovery can be much shorter, if we work at and desire it. God the Holy Spirit is able to restore us to sanity or wholeness through the good grieving process in less than seven years, even a little as days.

It is highly recommended that you visit the following website for important information on grief. While the information is written for an audience of professionals in the field, insight can be received to benefit those who mourn.

> http://www.ncbi.nlm.nih.gov/pmc/articles/PMC2691160/
> **Grief and Bereavement: What Psychiatrists Need to Know**
> World Psychiatry, 2009 June; 8(2): 67-74
> Sidney Zisook and Katherine
> Department of Psychiatry, University of California at San Diego

From your three (3) lists, please combine the names of deceased and living persons for whom you grieve, and catastrophic events or losses that grieve you the most on the following page. Total the number of years to see how compounded your grief is. Can you afford to keep that level of pain in your life? Grief attracts more grief. If you are ready to be healed, beside each, write "HTH" which stands for Heal the Hurt as your prayer to heal and to reclaim your soul. Seal the prayer with In Jesus Name! Amen. You have the authority to use His Name!

_____ _____

_____ _____

_____ _____

_____ _____

_____ _____

_____ _____

_____ _____

_____ _____

Lay It Down or Breakdown? CHOOSE!

Consider this. You bought a sleek, muscle car that is absolutely gorgeous on the outside. It is in perfect, brand new condition. However, eventually, the windshield wipers stop working, so you can't see in the rain. Then, the transmission starts acting up. So, it's not shifting properly, especially at high speeds. You turn on the air conditioner and it's blowing out hot air. You attempt to roll down the windows, but they don't work. You stop at the red light, and your car cuts off.   You try to crank it, but it just groans. You pray and ask God to just get the car started and you will go straight home. Finally, it starts. You head home. Just as you pull in the driveway, the car stops, again. You hear this strange decompression kind of sound that tells you something is really wrong. The computer system just clunked out, completely. Your transmission is shot; and your motor just blew up. Is your car broken down? Absolutely! Your car is not working.

Believe it or not, Christians have meltdowns or breakdowns, also. The problem is that many wear masks. Therefore, they grieve in silence or shame as if there is something wrong with admitting the truth. Statistics that reflect the number of people in the United States with some form of mental illness are staggering.   Believe it or not, those statistics include Christians. Grief can be a major contributor to meltdowns, mental illness, and emotional breakdowns.

To be spiritually, mentally, physically, and emotionally healthy is necessary if we are to obey God's Commandment to love God, love ourselves, and love our neighbor. We are taught and learned that the more we go to church, the more whole, spiritually healthy, and mature we become. That is not necessarily true, if we are filled with negative emotions, too ashamed to acknowledge our hurt, and refuse to seek help! We should voluntarily choose to surrender every aspect of our lives and brokenness to God for healing, delivery, recovery, and restoration.

To recover from or prevent meltdown or breakdown, we lay all the things we attempt to juggle in life at the feet of Jesus. The inability to manage all the various obligations in our lives may cause grief also. The following exercise is designed as a starting point. Lay it down at the feet of Jesus in prayer! Let go!

Randomly list the main obligations that you are attempting to juggle in your life.

_____   _____

_____   _____

_____   _____

_____   _____

_____   _____

Describe for yourself how successful you feel you are at making everything work.

_____

_____

_____

_____

What do you feel would be the result if all the balls you have in the air came crashing to the ground?

_____

_____

_____

_____

What would be the difference between a physical or emotional crash or breakdown and voluntarily surrendering everything to God for direction?

_____

_____

_____

_____

_____

At some point, in some way, either some or all of the things you were attempting will fell apart. The unexpected crash is a lot more devastating than releasing everything to God to eliminate some things, set in order what is left, prioritize and order your steps. In other words, change your perspective or frame of reference.

Decide not just to heal from the past hurt, but also to prevent an impending crash. That could bring enormous grief from which more recovery will be necessary. As you facilitate your recovery from the past crashes and hurt, submit all the balls you have in the air to God, voluntarily. Please pray this prayer!

Prayer!

"Holy God! You are grace, power, wonder and order! Please help me to prioritize my life, according to Your perfect will. I surrender it all to You. I ask that You order my thoughts, steps, actions, and responses in everything, everyday!"

In the Name of Jesus!
Amen!

NEW PRIORITIES

CHRIST/ Spiritual Walk

_____

_____

_____

Family / Relationships

_____

_____

_____

Finances/Resources

_____

_____

_____

Career / Education

_____

_____

_____

Plans/Opportunities

_____

_____

_____

Future / Uncertainties

_____

_____

_____

3.10 – SOUL SEARCH!

The soul and spirit are what we will need to enter eternal life in heaven. So, perhaps for the first time in your life, let's examine some qualities and characteristics of the soul, based upon the Holy Bible.

Please read the following scriptures. Please write a brief thought, prayer request to God, or commentary concerning your need for Godly soul characteristics, based upon the scripture provided. Notice the close relationship between the Word and the soul. Psalm 119 is the longest Psalm. Throughout it, the Word and soul align.

Leviticus 20:6 – "And the soul that turneth after such as have familiar spirits, and after wizards, to go a whoring after them, I will even set my face against that soul, and will cut him off from among his people."

_____

_____

_____

_____

Psalm 119:25 - "My soul cleaveth unto the dust: quicken (make alive) thou me according to thy word."

_____

_____

_____

_____

Psalm 119:28 - "My soul melteth for heaviness: strengthen thou me according unto thy word."

_____

_____

_____

_____

Psalm 119:81 - "My soul fainteth for thy salvation: but I hope in thy word."

_____

_____

_____

_____

Psalm 119:109 - "My soul is continually in my hand: yet do I not forget thy law."

_____

_____

_____

_____

_____

Psalm 119:129 - "Thy testimonies are wonderful: therefore doth my soul keep them."

_____

_____

_____

_____

_____

Matthew 16:26 - "For what is a man profited, if he shall gain the whole world, and lose his own soul? Or what shall a man give in exchange for his soul?"

_____

_____

_____

_____

_____

I Peter 1:22 – "Seeing ye have purified your souls in obeying the truth through the Spirit unto unfeigned love of the brethren, see that ye love one another with a pure heart fervently:"

_____

_____

_____

_____

_____

Hebrews 10:39 – "But we are not of them who draw back unto perdition; but of them that believe to the saving of the soul."

_____

_____

_____

_____

Psalm 23:3 – "He restoreth my soul: he leadeth me in the path of righteousness for his name's sake."

_____

_____

_____

_____

From Psalm 23:3, what relationship do you see between God's restoration of the soul and God leading us IN the path of righteousness?

_____

_____

_____

_____

SOUL Food!

Psalm 119:16 – "My soul hath kept thy testimonies; and I love them exceedingly".

Psalm 120:2 – "Deliver my soul, O LORD, from lying lips, and from a deceitful tongue."

Psalm 120:6 – "My soul hath long dwelt with him that hateth peace."

Psalm 121:7 – "The Lord shall preserve thee from all evil: He shall preserve thy soul."

Psalm 123:4 – "Our soul is exceedingly filled with the scorning of those that are at ease, and with the contempt of the proud."

Psalm 124:4 – "Then the waters had overwhelmed us, the stream had gone over our soul: Then the proud waters had gone over our soul."

Psalm 124:7 – "Our soul is escaped as a bird out of the snare of the fowlers: the snare is broken, and we are escaped."

Psalm 130:5 – "I wait for the LORD, my soul doth wait, and in His word do I hope."

Psalm 130:6 – "My soul waiteth for the Lord more than they that watch for the morning: I say, more than they that watch for the morning."

Psalm 138:3 – "In the day when I cried thou answeredst me, and strengthenedst me with strength in my soul."

Psalm 139:14 – "I will praise thee; for I am fearfully and wonderfully made: marvelous are thy works; and that my soul knoweth right well."

Below, please write a personal reflection on the importance of your own soul-care based on reading the above Psalms.

_____

_____

_____

_____

_____

_____

_____

_____

_____

3.11 – SOUL PROSPERTITY = TOTAL PROSPERITY!

3 John 1:2 – "Beloved, I wish above all things that thou may prosper and be in health, even as thy soul prospers."

The gold bullions in the image above symbolize wealth in the secular world. We use it as an image to represent true, legitimate, spiritual prosperity or spiritual wealth that is available to every Christian. It is the only lasting wealth or prosperity that exists. We prosper only as our souls prosper. If you believe you prosper from the reclaiming of your soul from all the places where it was scattered, the cleansing and alignment with the will of God, declare all areas where you now prosper in your life, as God the Holy Spirit reveals! Do not deviate! Hold to your faith in Jesus Christ who created all things for your good and secured our salvation.

AS MY SOUL PROSPERS, I PROSPER IN THE FOLLOWING AND ALL THINGS!

_____ _____

_____ _____

_____ _____

_____ _____

_____ _____

_____ _____

Please repeat the following prayer aloud!

Jehovah Rapha: I believe Isaiah 53:5. The stripes that Jesus received on His way to the cross also healed my soul. I live in faith to see the manifestation of that healing. I have endured. Now, I reclaim my soul for You from every place that it is scattered. I believe that my soul is saved. Therefore, it is whole. I live in full abundance with my soul that prospers in Your Word. The cares of this world don't distract me. You are God alone. My soul worships You – the True and Living God - alone! In You, I remain victorious as I live in obedience to You!

In the Name of Jesus,
Amen!

What benefit to you and your relationship with God do you expect to experience from **setting a watch** over your soul, so that it is not scattered in the future?

_____

_____

_____

_____

_____

_____

Please describe what it means to you for your soul to prosper?

_____

_____

_____

_____

_____

How will you intentionally love God differently with your whole soul in place?

_____

_____

_____

_____

_____

_____

3.12 – SPIRIT AND SOUL!

GOD'S BREATH IS LIFE!

Nephesh is the Hebrew word for the Breath of God. It is written:

Genesis 2:7 – "And the Lord God formed man of the dust of the ground, and breathed into his nostrils the breath of life; and man became a living soul."

Pneuma is the Greek word for the Breath of God. It is written:

John 20:21-22 – "Then said Jesus to them again, Peace be unto you: as my Father hath sent me, even so send I you. And when he had said this, he breathed on them, and saith unto them, Receive ye the Holy Ghost:"

Acts 2:2 – "And suddenly there came a sound from heaven as of a rushing mighty wind, and it filled all the house where they were sitting."

The above image is an erupting volcano. It was chosen because it represents in a limited way the unlimited magnitude of the Breath of God. We ponder the thought that a power greater than all the volcanoes in the world combined, and more, was inbreathed into the first Adam and "man became a living soul" without destroying him. In Genesis 1 and 2 God spoke everything into existence. With God's voice, God created the whole world and everything in it. In Genesis 2:7, the breath of God – the Nephesh – creates the soul in Adam. The Breath of God in us gives us new life, and unlimited power to do God's will.

Jesus breathed on the disciples that included more than just the 11 original disciples. As a result, they received God the Holy Spirit prior to Pentecost. God the Holy Spirit empowered them to wait for Pentecost and to share the gospel.

Science proves that molecules that are breathed into the atmosphere remain in the atmosphere. I imagine in my mind and believe in my soul that the sons and daughters of God are able to exclusively receive both a tiny particle of the breath that Jesus breathed, as the Son of God and the Son of man; and God the Holy Spirit for new life.

On the Internet site that is presented below, Rees Sloan presents a statistical analysis of the percentage of a molecule of breath of everyone whoever breathed that is still in the air. He incorporates Jesus into the presentation analysis. What makes his presentation even more credible is that Sloan makes no claims to be a Christian. Please see the following site, just to stimulate your thoughts. It gives some very impactful thoughts, and God's power.

http://www.warrior-scholar.com/smf/index.php?topic=744.0;wap2

If you believe it is true that molecules of the breath of Jesus are still in the atmosphere, what does that mean to you? Think a little more deeply than normal. Smile!

_____

_____

_____

_____

_____

In Acts 2:7 of the New Testament, the Pneuma, the Breath of God the Holy Spirit, enters as a "rushing mighty wind". In that instance, God the Holy Spirit enters the earth to indwell believers from that point forward, according to Acts 2:17. The Holy Spirit re-creates and empowers those who accept Jesus as Savior.

If God the Holy Spirit has an unlimited range of power, consider what happened to those who were broken because of Jesus' crucifixion and ascension. How do you think that day at Pentecost changed their hurt into wholeness?

_____

_____

_____

_____

_____

We know that God the Holy Spirit is the Third Person of the Godhead who formed and yet maintains the Church and us. God the Holy Spirit is a Person and not some disembodied spirit without form or substance.

What is your perception of God the Holy Spirit's power to work in you to heal your hurt and restore you to wholeness?

_____

_____

_____

God the Holy Sprit changes our spirit to be holy like the holy image of the perfect invisible God. The beauty in the original creation and the salvation process of re-creation is that the unlimited power of God's breath is breathed in such a way that it creates and re-creates without destroying the vessel – you and me. God the Holy Spirit yet continues to enable us to "do all things through Christ who strengthens us".

Look at the volcano erupting, again. What difference does it make in your life to know that God the Holy Spirit dwells in you in full bodily form with power (Greek – DUNAMIS) that is greater than all the volcanoes, power, bombs, and nuclear facilities in the world combined?

_____

_____

_____

_____

_____

How will you work with the power of God the Holy Spirit within you to re-create you as the spiritual image of God to benefit the Church of Jesus Christ and you?

_____

_____

_____

_____

_____

3.13 – GOD'S SPIRIT CREATES LIFE!
GOD'S SPIRIT RE-CREATES LIFE!

I Corinthians 15:45 – "And so it is written, the first man Adam was made a living soul; the last Adam was made a quickening spirit."

Stay with us. God has something important to say. We circle around to pick up some Biblical truths already mentioned to strengthen the frame of reference.

We encourage you to take another very serious look at how God created us and how God the Holy Spirit re-creates us. Sons and daughters of God are a re-creation through God the Holy Spirit. When we are re-created, we become co-laborers/co-creators with God the Holy Spirit and other believers to share life-giving truths of God.

Therefore, it is important to understand the power of God's Spirit that is available to believers to manifest total spiritual and emotional healing. Jesus died, resurrected, and ascended after He declared "all power is in my hand" (Matthew 28:20). Jesus will return to receive those who spiritually look like Him! Our goal is the truth in I John 3:2! We will look like Jesus! Jesus is clutter free!

Remember this:

- Everyone has a human spirit that is the natural or carnal spirit. The natural or carnal spirit is the one with which we were born. It is not yet submitted to the power of God the Holy Spirit for change and transformation to holiness. The natural or carnal spirit wars against our rebirth or regeneration.

- Born-Again Christians have a regenerate spirit that is a supernatural spirit. The inner person is re-created to the holy image of God through the daily process of salvation called regeneration.

As servants of God, we are to imitate Jesus Christ to do greater works, according to John 14:12. How will you use the Breath of God in you as a born-again Christian to speak life, health and healing in your life, and the lives of others?

_____

_____

_____

_____

_____

_____

3.14 – GOD'S DIVINE DESIGN FOR HEALING!

You are encouraged to greatly expand your knowledge and perception of the limitless power of the one, True God. God declares that if we seek God we will find God when we seek with all of our heart. Deep exploration of the scripture leads us to search extra-Biblical data in ancient documents, books, and now the Internet to seek to know more about God. The result is that we expand our love for God; our amazement about God; and our service to God. The results are always astounding revelations straight from God. Such is the result of research of the symbol above. God reveals God's self to us in such a way that there is no doubt that God is God. The revelations are often especially poignant because many who were formerly atheists or those who sought to disprove the existence of the God of Jesus Christ often end their search as born-again Christians.

From the Fall of Man in the Garden of Eden to the Birth of Christ, the Crucifixion, Resurrection, Ascension, and soon Return (Parousia) of Jesus Christ, we see clearly that God always has (always present tense) an eternal plan for the salvation of humankind that includes health and healing of all kinds. The plan is Christ. For example, with the invention of modern technology, it was discovered that as the Israelites marched through the wilderness for 40 years, they marched in the formation of the cross. The shape was a foursquare cross of human formation, with all four (4) points on the compass.

Perhaps you wonder what is the relevance of this fact to healing your hurt? The answer is that everything that ever occurred is displayed in the Word of God. Everything is connected to God's divine plan for your salvation. Please visit the following website, even if you don't read the entire document or understand it. What you will see is how the cross formation was the pattern of the wilderness journey for the Israelites. There was a gigantic human cross in the wilderness. Please see the following website for more insight.

http://www.biblewheel.com/wheel/spokes/Dalet_cross.asp
Spoke 4 - Dalet - The Foursquare Camp in the ... - **BibleWheel**.com

It is written:

Exodus 15:26 – "...If thou wilt diligently hearken to the voice of the Lord thy God, and wilt do that which is right in his sight, and wilt give ear to his commandments, and keep all his statutes, I will put none of these diseases upon thee, which I have brought upon the Egyptians: for I am the Lord that healeth thee."

Numbers 21:8-9 – "And the Lord said unto Moses, make thee a fiery serpent, and set it upon a pole: and it shall come to pass, that every one that is bitten, when he looketh upon it, shall live. And Moses made a serpent of brass, and put it upon a pole, and it came to pass, that if a serpent had bitten any man, when he beheld the serpent of brass, he lived."

In Exodus 15:26, God makes a binding Covenant of Healing with the Israelites, and us. God introduces God's self as Jehovah-Rapha – the God Who Heals. The Covenant is all-inclusive of spiritual, physical, and emotional health that includes the healing of our hearts, souls, and minds. Because of Christ, we have a better Covenant. The illnesses of the enemy will not come upon us. God promises!

Describe what the Covenant of Healing in Exodus 15:26 in conjunction with Isaiah 53:5 and Matthew 25:26 really means to you regarding physical, emotional and spiritual health.

_____

_____

_____

Numbers 21:8-9 states God's instruction to Moses to make an image to heal the Israelites when the deadly poisonous snakes bit them. They were bitten because of sin and disobedience. Nevertheless, we yet see God's compassion and grace toward them to heal them.

The instruction to Moses for this healing instrument is interesting because of God's commandment in Exodus 20:4 not to create graven images. However, we understand this to be a foreshadowing or typology of Christ on the cross. I suggest that it is, as well, a symbol of victory over the subtle quality of satan that Genesis 3:1 one describes. Jesus is the victory of Genesis 3:16 over the serpent.

Over time, the symbol of the serpent on a pole became a part of Greek mythology, commerce and trade. Later, the medical profession used the image of a serpent on a pole to represent healing. The previous image is a stylized version of that symbol for the medical profession in North America. Little do most know that the image or icon is Bible-based.

What simple idea about healing your hurt do you now think for the first time?

_____

_____

_____

_____

Based on this modern day symbol of healing, how do you see what God instructed Moses to do as a part of God's plan to heal your hurt?

_____

_____

_____

_____

_____

How will you look at the symbol of medicine differently going forward when you see it in your physician's office or elsewhere?

_____

_____

_____

_____

In what way or ways do you need to change your thinking about the true God as Jehovah-Rapha, the God Who Heals everything concerning you? (Remember! Jesus finished it!)

_____

_____

_____

_____

_____

_____

When Jesus was lifted up on the cross, it was the completion of God's eternal divine design that is previewed in Numbers 21:8-9 as a type or typology. Every time you see the medical icon or symbol in a doctors office, even if there is no cross there, God speaks.

LOOK UP! Use your imagination to see Jesus on the cross. Believe God has healed your hurt and delivers you from all the pain of your past.

3.15 – GOD'S SIGNATURE!

Psalm 19:1 – "The heavens declare the glory of God; and the firmament sheweth his handiwork."

Romans 1:20 – "For the invisible things of Him from the creation of the world are clearly seen, being understood by the things that are made, even His eternal power and Godhead; so that they are without excuse:"

God places God's signature on everything that God created. In fact, God yet speaks that all of God's creation is good. Romans 1:20 is particularly engaging in this portion of the presentation as we connect some dots. Let me explain what is intended.

Around 1979, scientists made an amazing discovery. That discovery is called laminin. Laminin is a protein molecule found in humans and animals. Basically, laminin holds and connects all of the cells in our body together. Let's connect the previous information to the discovery of laminin.

As God the Holy Spirit revealed, we observe that God created laminin before the foundation of the world, based on Romans 1:20. It really took the total course of human history to date for God to reveal this fact to humankind. When Moses placed the serpent on the rod, it was a foreshadowing or preview of Christ on the cross. Through the divine providence of God, laminin is shaped like a cross. The truth of Romans 1:20 is clearly evident. Laminin is God's signature of creation within every human being, "so that they are without excuse" to know God. Inside every being in the Animal Kingdom are countless, critical cross-shaped protein molecules. For me, they are God's Signature in us.

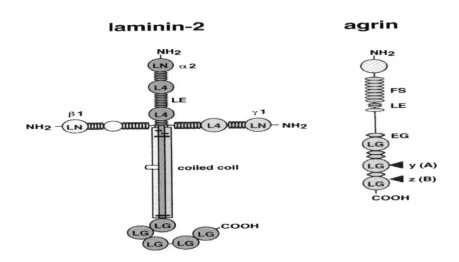

For additional study about laminin, please Google "structure of laminin" on the Internet.

How do you see the relationship between the Covenant of Healing, the serpent image that Moses constructed; the Christ on the cross: the medical symbol; and laminin as God's healing and recovery design for you in all areas of your spirit, soul, mind and body? Do you believe it is all connected to God's best for you?

_____

_____

_____

_____

_____

_____

Christ is the Healer. He designed and desires our total wholeness. What excuses do you make now or have you made in the past for resisting the emotional healing of Christ?

_____

_____

_____

_____

_____

God's designed you with great attention to every detail, including laminin. How should God's attention to detail in creating and re-creating you influence how you respond in detail to God's commandment to love God with all your heart, soul, and mind?

_____

_____

_____

_____

_____

_____

3.16 – GOD'S IMAGE AND INTEGRITY ARE HOLY!

Leviticus 20:7 – " Sanctify yourselves therefore, and be ye holy: for I am the Lord your God."

1 Peter 1:15 - 16 – "But as He which hath called you is holy, so be ye holy in all manner of conversation; Because it is written, be ye holy; for I am holy."

God is holy. God commands us to be holy. To be holy requires that WE SANCTIFY OURSELVES. In other words, we intentionally, deliberately, and passionately set ourselves apart from the world, unto the Lord, for the work of God the Holy Spirit in us. Building the holy character of God in us is linked to setting ourselves apart. Pursue God's revelation of who God is and God's righteousness. Healing our hurt makes everything a lot simpler.

God the Holy Spirit who lives in us is the full, holy, powerful and complete Third Person of the Trinity – the Godhead – Who is God the Father; God the Son; God the Holy Spirit. We sanctify ourselves or we set ourselves apart from the world and our carnal nature unto God. The Holy Spirit makes us over in the holy image of God that was lost at the Fall of Humankind in the Garden of Eden.

In meditation and prayer, closely examine the following scriptures. They present a few examples of the need to actively set ourselves apart for God on a continuous basis; and to seek God through prayer, meditation, service and worship. To do so is our surrendered commitment to the process of sanctification and regeneration.

It is written:

Joshua 3:5 – "And Joshua said unto the people, sanctify yourselves: for tomorrow the Lord will do wonders among you."

I Corinthians 1:30 – "But of Him you are in Christ Jesus, who became for us wisdom from God—and righteousness and sanctification and redemption"

What was the responsibility of the people in Joshua 3:5?

_____

_____

_____

_____

_____

What does Joshua 3:5 say God would do after the Israelites sanctified themselves?

_____

John 17:19 – "And for their sakes I sanctify myself, that they also might be sanctified through the truth."

If God the Holy Spirit is making us over to be like Christ, what does this example in Jesus' high priestly prayer teach us about the need to sanctify ourselves?

_____

_____

_____

_____

I Peter 3:15 – "But sanctify the Lord God in your hearts: and be ready always to give an answer to every man that asketh you a reason of the hope that is in you with meekness and fear:"

Please write a brief commentary based on what God the Holy Spirit speaks to you about I Peter 3:15.

_____

_____

_____

Psalm 14:2 – "The Lord looked down from heaven upon the children of men, to see if there were any that did understand, and seek God."

Based on Psalm 14:2 and Psalm 53:2, when the Lord looks down from heaven to see if there are any that understand and seek God, how will your "understanding" and "seeking" represent you as a disciple of Jesus Christ?

_____

_____

_____

_____

Psalm 27:4 – "One thing have I desired of the Lord, that will I seek after; that I may dwell in the house of the Lord all the days of my life, to behold the beauty of the Lord, and to enquire in his temple."

What is the one spiritual thing pertaining to your heart, soul, and mind that you desire of the Lord, seek after and sanctify yourself?

_____

_____

_____

_____

I Thessalonians 5:23 – "And the very God of peace sanctify you wholly; and I pray God your whole spirit and soul and body be preserved blameless unto the coming of our Lord Jesus Christ."

Describe how you see this scripture as one to which you should aspire?

_____

_____

_____

_____

Hebrews 11:16 – "But without faith it is impossible to please him: for he that cometh to God must believe that he is, and that he is a rewarder of them that diligently seek him."

What does this scripture teach you about faith, the benefits of "persistently" seeking God and sanctifying yourself?

_____

_____

_____

_____

_____

_____

3.17 – GOD THE HOLY SPIRIT CHANGES OUR SPIRIT AND SOUL!

Nothing on earth could ever do justice to the power of God. However, these images are feeble attempts that are used to represent the Spiritual attribute of who God is and who we are in Christ. Like the volcano presented earlier, the tallest plume of smoke above can represent God the Holy Spirit's range of power that works in us, with us, through us, and on our behalf. For the sake of our discussion, the larger smokestack represents the unlimited power of God the Holy Spirit. The smaller smokestack represents how the Christian spirit is transformed to be in the holy image of God through the processes of salvation.

Create an image in your mind that you would use to describe the presence of God the Holy Spirit in your life. Please write the description of your image below.

_____

_____

_____

_____

_____

It is written:

James 4:14 – "...What is your life? It is even a vapor that appeareth for a little time then vanisheth away."

Based on James 4:14, the image of the smokestacks can represent our spirits or life – which is a vapor like steam. It can also represent how we become one with God the Holy Spirit as Jesus prayed for us to do in His High Priestly Prayer that John 17 records. As God removes harmful hurt, room is made for our increased focus on our spiritual transformation. The three baptisms immerse us in Christ; fitly join us together as the Body of Christ through God the Holy Spirit; and identify us as the beloved sons and daughters of God.

What is your response to reading the blessing of divine unity of your spirit and soul with God that John 17 describes?

_____

_____

_____

_____

The more we submit to God and live in accordance with God's Word, the more our spirit is changed to be like God's Spirit – Holy. Ultimately, there should be no separation between the Spirit of God and us. We become one when our spirit is fused or united with Jesus. That takes work on our part. Jesus did and yet does His part.

Describe how important it is to continue to surrender control of your life to God the Holy Spirit for daily transformation.

_____

_____

_____

_____

_____

The other smokestacks in the backgrounds could easily represent how God the Holy Spirit unifies the Body of Christ. Through God the Holy Spirit, those who are in the Church of Jesus Christ are unified as a single, saved Body who is one!

3.18 – GOD THE HOLY SPIRIT: THE PRESENT PRESENCE OF THE GODHEAD!

Since Pentecost, God the Holy Spirit is the Third Person of the Godhead who is present with us. The Holy Spirit forms the church, indwells the sons and daughters of God, and transforms us to the image of God the Son!

Acts 1:8 – "But ye shall receive power, after that the Holy Ghost is come upon you: and ye shall be witnesses unto me both in Jerusalem, and in all Judaea, and in Samaria, and unto the uttermost part of the earth."

Based on Act 1:8, God the Holy Spirit empowers you to be a witness about the salvation of Jesus Christ. Describe how you will be a more effective witness for Christ after healing your hurt!

_____

_____

_____

_____

_____

_____

_____

Acts 2:39 – "For the promise is unto you, and to your children, and to all that are afar off, even as many as the Lord our God shall call."

How do you see the fulfilled promise of God the Holy Spirit as your present working power source to facilitate your spiritual growth and healing?

_____

_____

_____

_____

_____

_____

It is written:

Psalm 34:3 – "O magnify the Lord with me, and let us exalt his name together."

God is NEVER less than God. We are required to enlarge OUR perception of God in US, in heaven and the universe. We pray to God the Father, through Jesus the Son, by the power of God the Holy Spirit who tells us for what we should pray, according to Romans 8:26. Right? Right!

So, we understand that we who are mere mortals CAN NEVER enlarge God. It is impossible. God is already greater than our human minds or spiritual ability can ever comprehend in totality. Therefore, what Psalm 34:3 teaches us is that we must push ourselves beyond our limits to magnify or expand our view and understating of who God is as God the Holy Spirit works with us, in us and through us. Our imagination must expand like a telescopic lens to ever increase our God perspective!

How will you deliberately magnify God the Holy Spirit as you go forward?

_____

_____

_____

_____

_____

Read John 14 – 17. Describe new insights and revelations that you receive about God the Holy Spirit.

_____

_____

_____

_____

_____

_____

_____

_____

3.19 – USE BORN-AGAIN AUTHORITY!

Matthew 10:1 – "And when he had called unto him his twelve disciples, he gave them power against unclean spirits, to cast them out, and to heal all manner of sickness and all manner of disease."

What does this power that Jesus also gave to you really mean to your deliverance from or protection against ungodly spirits, sickness, diseases, and hurt?

_____

_____

_____

_____

Luke 10:19 – "Behold, I give unto you power to tread on serpents and scorpions, and over all the power of the enemy: and nothing shall by any means hurt you."

Look at the range of power that you have through Jesus Christ. How do you apply that to your life in Christ and your healing?

_____

_____

_____

_____

John 1:12 – "But as many as received him, to them gave the power to become the sons of God, even to them that believe on his name:"

Jesus gives you the power to become the sons and daughters of God. How will your Kingdom authority impact the world for Christ when you are healed?

_____

_____

_____

_____

3.20 – IMAGINATION!

"Imagination is more important than knowledge. For knowledge is limited to all we now know and understand, while imagination embraces the entire world, and all there ever will be to know and understand." - Albert Einstein

God gave us five senses (sight, hearing, touch, taste, smell) AND imagination for a reason! Everything that exists is the result of someone's imagination – good, bad or otherwise. Spiritual creative imagination for the good of the Kingdom of God, the world, and us is grossly underused. Each of us can and should use imagination significantly more and better! It is the great creative component of who we are as humans.

Just as all five natural senses inform our perception of the natural world, our spirits have five senses of perception that inform the spirit being. Imagination requires us to use the spiritual senses to see beyond the natural to the supernatural dimension. There, we see what does not yet exist in the natural, and other things could be improved for the greater good of all.

I submit to you that imagination is priceless as a mechanism to "magnify" the Lord or enlarge our perception of who God is. Imagination is a component of the soul that is improved through creative use! God speaks to us there, as well, and will show us new and endless possibilities. Work your imagination for greater works. Some things are missing in the world and waiting for you to imagine something new.

I heard a statistic once that said less than 3% of people imagine one new thing a year. That is what we really call missing the mark. Look at the image above. Use your spiritual imagination to briefly describe what that image could become. Be a kid for a moment. Improve the image with your imagination and crayons.

_____

_____

_____

_____

Imagine God working on your behalf every second of every day of your life – past, present, and future! What do you see or imagine?

_____

_____

_____

_____

_____

Imagine heaven! Describe what you see, hear, touch, taste, and smell!

_____

_____

_____

_____

_____

Imagine yourself as a finished product – fully blessed! Describe below how you look spiritually, mentally, and physically!

_____

_____

_____

_____

_____

_____

_____

_____

_____

Imagine living without hurt, fear, shame, or guilt. How does that feel? Please describe your feelings below. Then accept it and live it, in the Name of Jesus!

_____

_____

_____

_____

_____

_____

Imagine something new and unique! Please describe what your senses tell you!

_____

_____

_____

_____

How will you incorporate your positive, Godly imagination into your daily living now?

_____

_____

_____

_____

_____

Since you have imagined all of that, work with God the Holy Spirit to DO it or BE it.

3.21 – VISIONING!

Imagine that this is the same blank face from the previous image. We challenge you to learn to bring your imagination to life with visioning. Visioning takes the basic form of what God reveals and adds embellishments, based on revelations. Those embellishments include dimension, color, flavor, and everything that God reveals to you regarding what God permitted you to imagine in the first place. HA!

Visioning requires use of the five senses of the spirit. It is easier to accomplish what you can imagine if you permit God the Holy Spirit to expand the basic concept. Patiently permit revelation from God to enter your soul and provide you with the details through visioning.

Suggested Process!

1. Read the Holy Bible and pray to see what God reveals. JOURNAL!
2. Sit quietly in meditation. Soft music without vocals is recommended.
3. Don't let the darkness disturb you. It will become the canvass.
4. Resist the urge to break your concentration on God and God's revelations!
5. See that heaven you imagined earlier with God on the throne and Jesus on the right hand of God interceding for you. (Smile!)
6. Believe that God the Holy Spirit is working with you and prompting you.
7. Talk to God within you with your thoughts. God hears you!
8. Remain in that state of seeking as long as God directs or possible.
9. Return to that place where you left off each time you are interrupted or stop.
10. Make imagining/visioning a daily practice and write/draw what is revealed.

3.22 – WRITE THE VISION!!

Habakkuk 2:1-3

"I will stand upon my watch, and set me upon the tower, and will watch to see what he will say unto me, and what I shall answer when I am reproved. And the LORD answered me, and said, Write the vision, and make it plain upon tables, that he may run that readeth it. For the vision is yet for an appointed time, but at the end it shall speak, and not lie: though it tarry, wait for it; because it will surely come, it will not tarry."

Get in Position to Receive the Vision!

SEE what God says. That is visioning. Write what you see from what you hear. When it is written, as a result of imagination and visioning, then you are able to focus your spiritual energy on that person, place, or thing to bring forth the vision. Provision is never the issue. God is the Source for the provision. PEOPLE ARE RE- SOURCES GOD SENDS. If God gave you the vision, God has already provided what is needed to bring it to reality. Some of us have this image of a "thumb-twitting" God. According to scripture, our God, the True God, the God of Jesus Christ, made and accomplished everything you will ever need for life and life's ministry assignment. God has already accomplished everything for us.

Position yourself to "**see**" what God "**says**". Based on Habakkuk 2:1-3, the vision is first presented through the sense of hearing. We listen for God's still, small voice. God is the narrator. We take dictation or write down what God says and shows.

Remember! God already finished it. God gives us portions of the vision along the journey, as we are obedient. God adds to the vision when we make ourselves available to SEE THE VISION AS WE HEAR GOD'S VOICE.

"Cemeteries are silent cities where many unfulfilled dreams and visions lie
with people who died with hurt that was never healed." - Nawanna L. Miller - 2000

Please write "God's Vision" to you, for you, below, even if you have written it before. Embellish it through prayer, the power of God the Holy Spirit, and visioning. Take your time! Use your fives senses and your IMAGINATION. Push through the limitations YOU set! God is not limited in any way. God wants to reveal God's plan for you to you.

_____

_____

_____

_____

_____

_____

_____

_____

_____

_____

_____

_____

_____

_____

_____

_____

_____

_____

_____

_____

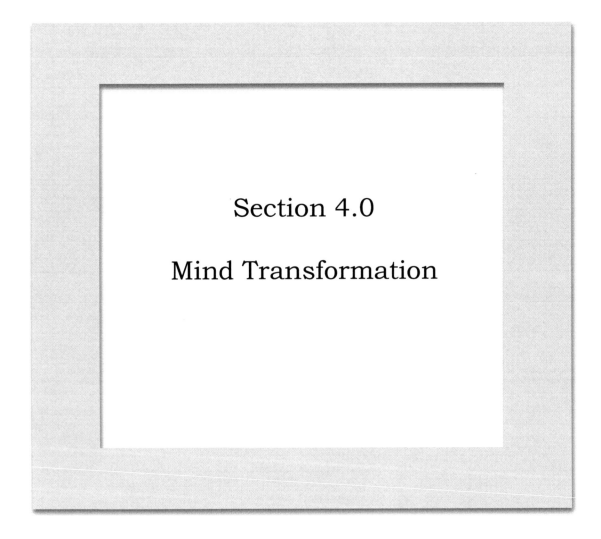

Section 4.0

Mind Transformation

4.1 – LOVE GOD WITH YOUR ENTIRE MIND!

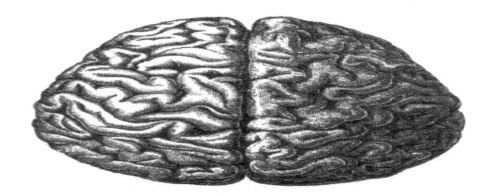

The brain is the most incredible, complex computer ever created. God folded it neatly inside our heads. God is smooth like that! It is the power center of the human body and controls all that a person thinks or does. That is an overwhelmingly phenomenal thought when we consider God's intricate design of the human brain. It controls every function of the body.

The mind is the seat of knowing. Some of the non-scholarly descriptions or concepts like mind blower, mind bender, mind altering, mind games, mind numbing, mind reader, mind trap, etc., serve to remind us of how important the mind is to our total existence and well-being.

Jesus commands us to love God with the entire mind. This commandment can be obeyed when we clear the clutter, including hurt, and every distracting thought that interrupts the flow of our love for God, God's love for us, and God's revelation to us. Like everything else in the Christian life, we must surrender our minds and thoughts to the Lord, intentionally.

Surrender of the mind to God may be very difficult because the old nature fights against you, and the will of God on the battlefield of the mind, first. Disciplined prayer and constant surrender are the keys to new habit formation, and a spiritual mind that is submitted to God. Based on Isaiah 26:3, our level of peace is direct evidence of whether our minds are focused on God, or something else. Love God with your entire mind! Trust God!

Remember! The first place the enemy attacks is the mind! Don't cooperate with that. Our sure defense against the attacks is the Word of God! What did God say? What does God the Holy Spirit reveal based upon the Word. Pray without ceasing for God's divine revelation. Think and believe the higher truths of God.

It is written:

Isaiah 26:3 – "Thou wilt keep him in perfect peace, whose mind is stayed on thee: because he trusteth in thee."

Please be honest with God and yourself. Describe below how you perceive the current condition of your mind!

_____

_____

_____

_____

_____

_____

_____

Based on the truth in Isaiah 26:3, how does your mind reflect the image of the perfect peace of God in your daily lifestyle?

_____

_____

_____

_____

_____

_____

Please name three thoughts you should change immediately and explain why!

_____

_____

_____

_____

_____

_____

4.2 – BATTLE OF THE MIND!

Romans 7:19-25 – "For the good that I would I do not: but the evil which I would not, that I do. Now if I do that I would not, it is no more I that do it, but sin that dwelleth in me. I find then a law, that, when I would do good, evil is present with me. For I delight in the law of God after the inward man: But I see another law in my members, warring against the law of my mind, and bringing me into captivity to the law of sin which is in my members. O wretched man that I am! who shall deliver me from the body of this death? I thank God through Jesus Christ our Lord. So then with the mind I myself serve the law of God; but with the flesh the law of sin."

There is a war going on within us. It is a war between the old, fleshly, carnal self and the spiritual person that we are becoming through the regeneration of God the Holy Spirit. Unfortunately, it is normal. Many people are unaware of that. Don't give up. We win through Christ when we persist in seeking the Christ-Mind!

The mind is the seat of intellectual authority. As a result, it is the battleground where wars are raged between the carnal and the spiritual self. It is the point of attack for the enemy. What we know intellectually is often at odds with the precepts of faith. Because it is third on the list in the First and Great Commandment, I suggest that the mind may very well be the more difficult to bring under subjection to the Spirit of God and our spirit than the heart and soul. The helmet of salvation reminds us of the need to place the mind under the spiritual authority of God the Holy Spirit.

4.3 – MENTAL FILE MODEL!

01 8934 1726 6934 8913 4490 3784 2314 4917 83
354 1890 7645 4320 5674 9809 8988 83921 4532
10290 45807 19100 1029 2314 288 938 3823 392
5588 90384 48882 329 0394 84750 0394 5892040
987 5948 3993 209 3094 259 3009 029485 6749 4
2988 492 8576 499 384 189 10202 4859 5770 384
34 3098 289 39393 20934 588 3984 03039940117
42 17 094 68 2983 837447 9485 5933 2983 99891
098 9403 400 998 0245 2039 89348 89938755932

As you have probably already guessed by now, this image was the inspiration for the cover of this workbook. During the seminar, it was shared how God gave me a night vision while sleeping that included what you see here and on the cover.

In the night vision, numbers like these were just floating upward into the air. They registered against a three-dimensional black velvet backdrop. This image is my best, though feeble effort, to reconstruct what I saw in that vision. When I asked God what that meant, God said, "These are all the memories and information that you no longer need." Seeking God has unbelievable unexpected benefits that we could never imagine on our own. Who knew God would do that?

God removed unnecessary stuff from my mind. The relief and freedom was incredible. God pressed DELETE! It felt like a heavy weight of matter was removed, but I didn't know what it was. The experience and lightness was such a joy. I went to bed before dark the next night and asked God to do it again! Smile! A year later, I watched the movie *The Matrix*. When I saw the numbers floating up, it was the same image from the vision. I was stunned. There is no such thing as coincidence. God handled every detail of our story. God is kind to let us know it.

Observe that this reconstructed image begins with the number one. We are the sum total of our experiences, each etched in our memory, from the first memory to the last. Whether good or bad, or whether we consciously remember what is stored in our brain or not, it's there. There is no way of knowing just how many files we have in our mind that the above image represents. It is true! Our thoughts determine everything about us – our decisions, appearance, character, success, future, plans, vision, relationships, and everything we do.

Do you have some corrupted files in your mind? Is it time to PRESS DELETE?

4.4 – MIND FILES!

Anger Abandonment Abuse Anxiety Addiction Abortion Age Ambition Brutality Bitterness Body Confusion Cussing Crisis Color Curses Coveting Divorce Death Depression Envy Eating Fear Failure Family Greed Guilt Hate Home Health Incest Incarceration Interests Job Jealousy Judging Kisses Lust Love Lies Life Money Molestation Miscarriages Misery Nation Needs Noise Oppression People Power Personalities Questions Rape Relationships Rejection Romance Retirement Sorrow Scars Security Situations Trouble Tests Trials Uncertainties Violence Worry X's Yearnings ZERO

God the Holy Spirit randomly gave me an idea of the range of negative words, thoughts, and experiences that the numbers on the cover and the previous image could represent in any one person's mind. The negative occupies valuable real estate in our heads. The list for our mental files is endless. Add to the list above.

What if we could or would examine the kinds of information that we carry around in our minds – on our brains. For everything the eye sees in millions of dots that form a portrait, the mind records. Imagine that. Much of it is useless details that we don't even remember seeing, much less can use to go forward.

What if we made a decision to optimize what goes in our minds/memories and thereby improve our brain function? What if we made a decision to think only Godly and creative thoughts? What if we believed and obeyed Colossians 3:1-3? I believe we would change our present circumstances and enhance our future!

THE CHOICE IS OURS. For example, anger is a choice! Deliberately and intentionally manage your emotions. Choose peace and blessedness instead! Take authority over your mind.

4.5 – MIND DUMP!

Through the power of God the Holy Spirit, we have the authority over our minds and our thoughts. Therefore, we have the power and authority to voluntarily decide what to keep and what to discard.

We DECIDE to think good or evil; victory or defeat. Prayer is critical to the process. Every since God showed me the vision, I greatly improved on what I permit to enter as the first line of defense for a healthy mind.

In the frame above, entitled The Mind Dump, quickly write single words about events/people that have your mind boggled down – good, bad, ugly, past, present or future. This includes the things that you too will no longer need going forward! You can't know everything that's in your mind, but this is a new beginning. Put as many single word thoughts in as possible, without overly thinking about them.

4.6 – WHAT'S ON YOUR MIND?

From the 4.5 Mind Dump image, select only the thoughts that are healthy and holy. Compile them in an orderly manner below. Ask God in prayer to remove the rest. Then press DELETE. Compare the results of your Christ Mind and your Natural Mind!

Christ-Mind!   **Natural Mind!**

_____   _____

_____   _____

_____   _____

_____   _____

_____   _____

_____   _____

_____   _____

_____   _____

_____   _____

Pray to God to remove from your mind everything that you will no longer need. From this point forward, make an agreement between God and you that negative thoughts can no longer take up residence in your mind. Stop them as soon as you sense the attempt at entry through your five senses and your imagination.

Habitually close the door on negative thoughts for good, every day, each time one arises. As much as possible, think the higher thoughts of God! God will add revelation to those Godly thoughts when the negative thoughts no longer reside.

RE-TRAIN YOUR MIND! RE-FRAME YOUR PORTRAIT OF LIFE!

4.7 – PLEASE DON'T FEED THE ANIMALS!

For years, I have used the phrase "Please don't feed the animals" to apply to spiritual warfare. Signs with that message are commonly used in places like the zoo. For me, the saying speaks of those spirits that we entertain in our lives that are not of God the Holy Spirit. Those ungodly spirits facilitate the war that is raged between the holy, spiritual person we are called to become as Christians, and the natural being that we were created. Eventually, the animals attack us; and we don't put up much resistance. Really!

I read the following tale on my nephew Steven Rushin's Facebook page. For some reason it spoke volumes to me as a way to explain the Biblical truth about the war within. Following is a shorter version of a longer tale.

An Old Cherokee Tale of Two Wolves - Author Unknown

One evening an old Cherokee Indian told his grandson about a battle that goes on inside people. He said, "My son, the battle is between two wolves inside us all. One is Evil. It is anger, envy, jealousy, sorrow, regret, greed, arrogance, self-pity, guilt, resentment, inferiority, lies, false pride, superiority, and ego. The other is good. It is joy, peace, love, hope, serenity, humility, kindness, benevolence, empathy, generosity, truth, compassion and faith."

The grandson thought about it for a minute and then asked his grandfather: "Which wolf wins?" The old Cherokee simply replied, "The one you feed".

Just as the Cherokee Tale was effective to explain the war within, the comment that was made as a point of view is just the statement that is needed to encourage you to place a value on what you think and feel. Use your Godly authority over your mind and spirit. The comment is included with my nephew's permission.

"Each and every one of us has these two wolves running around inside us. The evil wolf or the good wolf is fed daily by the choices we make with our thoughts. What you think about and dwell upon will in a sense appear in your life and influence your behavior."

"We have a choice to feed the Good Wolf and good will show up positively in our character, habits, and behavior. Or feed the Evil Wolf and our whole world will turn negative. Like poison, this will slowly eat away at our soul. The crucial question is: Which wolf are you feeding today?"

What are your thoughts regarding the Tale of Two Wolves as a metaphor for the war within?

_____

_____

_____

_____

_____

_____

_____

_____

Please describe how you will feed your inner spiritual person and mind with Godly thoughts and actions going forward, based upon the Word of God and God's personal revelations.

_____

_____

_____

_____

_____

_____

Consume more Word! The evil wolf will die from starvation!

4.8 – COMMANDMENT! RENEW YOUR MIND!

Romans 12:1-3 – "I beseech you therefore, brethren, by the mercies of God, that ye present your bodies a living sacrifice, holy, acceptable unto God, which is your reasonable service (worship). And be not conformed to this world: but be ye transformed by the renewing of your mind, that ye may prove what is that good, and acceptable, and perfect, will of God. For I say, through the grace given unto me, to every man that is among you, not to think of himself more highly than he ought to think; but to think soberly, according as God hath dealt to every man the measure of faith."

We are commanded to love God with our entire mind and present our bodies as living sacrifices on the altar of God. Let's stop squirming! Lay still in God's presence. Stay there in faith! If God commands it, that means God has provision in place to obey the commandment. God would not command us to do something that we could not do. One of the keys to obeying that commandment is embedded in Romans 12:1-3. "Renew your mind!"

Briefly describe the relationship between presenting our bodies as living sacrifices and the transformation of our minds?

_____

_____

_____

_____

_____

4.9 – SPIRIT AND SCIENCE OF MIND! TRANSFORMATION!

To expand the discussion on God's command to love God with all our mind is difficult because there is way too much that can and should be included. When we think about it, amassing knowledge and understanding of the brain/mind is the last superstructure frontier regarding the human body!

"Science is seeing God through what God created." That is what God said to me many years ago. There is no place that we can get a better glimpse of God than when we look at the science that attempts to explains the most intricately, phenomenal computer God made. We call it the brain. Like the soul and spirit, the brain and the mind are inseparable. God placed the brain with the mind in the hard container called the skull. Then God told us to put the helmet of salvation on it to protect it. What a divine Creator-God! We should be grateful that God didn't put our brains in our feet!

According to science, Neuroplasticity is the ability of the mind to resurface itself, like paving a dirt road or resurfacing a paved highway. The discovery was made in the last quarter of the 20th century. It is suggested that you conduct additional research on the fascinating study of Neuroplasticity.

When God commands us to be transformed by the renewing of our minds in Romans 12:1-3, Neuroplasticity is the mechanism God placed in our brains to make that possible, at the creation. Scientists just "discovered" it. God validated the revelation that if God told us to renew our minds, God made the means to do so available!

Recently, I was still in great search of a way to include in this study a better understanding of Neuroplasticity, the importance of healthy brain function, and the spiritual authority we should take over our brain. Through God's grace, after church one Sunday, God literally led me to a Public Television Broadcast that Dr. Daniel Amen presented. Dr. Amen is a neuroscientist who places before us the science needed to understand the command to renew our minds. The knowledge revealed was so amazing! I have become a student of Dr. Amen's teachings. Beside, I love the name. Please watch the following video:

@ http://www.youtube.com/watch?v=4M1iTalBcBg&feature=related
Brain and Aging, Use Your Brain to Change Your Age, Daniel G. Amen M.D.
www.amensolutions.com

Sit beyond the Veil with God. Jesus made that possible, too. Change your way of thinking, and the things about which you think. Change you life! What God the Holy Spirit is willing to teach us is unbelievable, at first. Beyond the Veil, God the Holy Spirit reveals to us the higher truths about God that are unspoken in casual encounters with God or buzz words!

147

It is possible that some suffer from a condition I call Lazy Minds. (It's a phrase I reworked from a comment one of our members, Hope Weatherspoon, made in Bible class regarding her magnificent voice that she described as lazy.) I suggest that Lazy Minds exist because of the unhealthy content that makes us mentally, and therefore spiritually, physically, emotionally, and intellectually sluggish. Lazy Minds are at war with the mind of the Spirit that is full of life, energy, revelation, power, wonder, truth, and more!

How will you use the ability of the brain to resurface itself to positively and spiritually improve the intellectual, spiritual and emotional input and output of your mind?

_____

_____

_____

_____

Proverbs 2:6 – "For the Lord giveth wisdom: out of his mouth cometh knowledge and understanding."

How will you seek and use the wisdom, knowledge, and understanding of God to change your mind to improve the context and content of your life, regularly?

_____

_____

_____

_____

_____

Proverbs 29:18 – "Where there is no vision, the people perish: but he that keepeth the law, happy is he."

How do you see visioning as a routine to improve the quality of your mind?

_____

_____

_____

_____

_____

Jeremiah 29:11 – "For I know the thoughts that I think toward you, saith the Lord, thoughts of peace, and not of evil, to give you an expected end."

In what ways will you think God's thoughts of peace and good that God thinks toward you to change your mind and improve your health?

_____

_____

_____

_____

_____

Matthew 27:51 – "And, behold, the veil of the temple was rent in twain from the top to the bottom; and the earth did quake, and the rocks rent;"

Because of Christ, you now have access beyond the Veil. What does the fact that you have unlimited access to God mean to your thought process?

_____

_____

_____

_____

_____

Philippians 3:20 – "For our conversation is in heaven; from whence also we look for the Savior, the Lord Jesus Christ:"

How do you perceive the conversation in heaven about you? Smile!

_____

_____

_____

_____

_____

To renew the mind, requires us to forget the impact of some things that hurt us. In other words, while it may remain in your mind, give no power or emotions to it. Now that you are working on forgiveness, let's consider another part of the same problem – forgetting. Many say, "God says forgive. God doesn't say we have to forget." Well! That is not true. And the mechanism – Neuroplasticity – is already in the brain to do just that. FORGET! Love, forgive and forget are action words.

It is written:

Philippians 3:13-14 – "Brethren, I count not myself to have apprehended: but this one thing I do, forgetting those things which are behind, and reaching forth unto those things which are before, I press toward the mark for the prize of the high calling of God in Christ Jesus."

Remember! This is a process! What do you need to do to reach forward?

_____

_____

_____

_____

_____

_____

What are the things for which you reach with your new Christ-Mind?

_____

_____

_____

_____

_____

_____

_____

4.10 – "I FORGET"

Following is a meditation based on Philippians 3:13-15 that is included in my book called **Cruising the Cosmos.** It is placed here merely to provide a sense of perspective on how forgetting can work for God's glory and our good.

I FORGET!

"Brethren, I count not myself to have apprehended: but this one thing I do, forgetting those things which are behind and reaching forth to those things which are before I press toward the mark for the prize of the high calling of God in Christ Jesus. Let us therefore, as many as be perfect, be thus minded: and if in anything you be otherwise minded, God shall reveal even this to you." (Philippians 3:13-15)

As I seek the perfect mind of Christ,
I release the past that had me bound.
The past can no longer block my way.
Though I am not perfect, yet,
My greatest testimony is: I forget.

There is so much more waiting for me.
From the past God has set me free.
In my future, there will not be this past.
Though I am not perfect, yet, I forget.

The high calling of Christ is high.
Blessings unlimited await me there, now.
I reach with all I have. I reach!
Since I seek His perfection,
Though I'm not perfect yet,
I forget.

What could be has not been so far.
As I press forward,
There is this joy that I now spot.
I didn't see it when I held to what was gone.
It only appeared to me when I left the past alone.
What might have been matters not.
The testimony of my survival is I forgot.

Though uncertain of my days ahead,
When all has been done,
And everything to say is said,
What I can't remember will not bother me.
The testimony is this of my life's journey.
I let it go. I forgot.

What I would have done is unchangeable now.
No need to squirm and furrow my brow.
No need to lament in sorrow, in tears.
No need to be immobilized because of fears.
I let it go. I forgot.

Whatever was, whatever could have been…
Whatever did or did not hap-pen,
By the clock…
I can't remember now since then
Because… I let it go!
I forgot!

Jesus dropped all my sin in the Sea of Forgetfulness.
He remembers it no more.
He never brings it up or throws it in my face.
That makes it possible to run this race.
If I want to be just like the Christ,
Sins against me must go there too.
So no longer will I remember the things
Done to me that inconsiderate others do.

No longer will I recall the past.
From that, I am free now at last.
I press through into the point of Light.
I press. When I forgot,
I found the God Place - True Blessedness.

I press through with hope - expectation.
I press.
Greater grace became my realization.
When I let go, I forgot.
I press through with Now Faith, never a doubt.
I press. When I forgot, God worked things out.

Ever True and Loving God:

Thank You for the sheer blessing of being able to renew my mind. I pray that I will let go of every thought that hinders me. I pray for Your strength in my weakness to press toward the mark for the prize of the high calling of God in Christ Jesus. I press through every distraction of my past to reach the plateau of your promises, fully assured of your Presence.

In the Name of Jesus!
Amen!

Philippians 2:4-6 – "Let this mind be in you, which was also in Christ Jesus:"

4.11 – RECEIVE THE MIND OF CHRIST!

Please use your imagination to think and describe below what it would be like to really embrace the thought that God commands us to receive the Christ-Mind.

_____

_____

_____

Philippians 4:6-7 – "Be careful for nothing; but in every thing by prayer and supplication with thanksgiving let your requests be made known unto God. And the peace of God, which passes all understanding, shall keep your hearts and minds through Christ Jesus."

Imagine total mental clarity based on the scripture above. AFFIRM the freedom and the luxury of the Christ-Mind! Begin each Affirmation with "I agree with Jesus that…!"

_____

_____

_____

Proverbs 9:11 – "For by me thy days shall be multiplied, and the years of thy life shall be increased."

Write an affirmation of this scripture from your brand new Christ-Mind!

_____

_____

Philippians 4:8 – "Finally, brethren, whatsoever things are true, whatsoever things are honest, whatsoever things are just, whatsoever things are pure, whatsoever things are lovely, whatsoever things are of good report; if there be any virtue, and if there be any praise, think on these things."

Write an affirmation of this scripture from your brand new Christ-Mind!

_____

_____

Mark 5:15 – " And they come to Jesus, and see him that was possessed with the devil, and had the legion, sitting, and clothed, and in his right mind: and they were afraid."

Write an affirmation of Mark 5:15 from your brand new Christ-Mind.

_____

_____

_____

_____

_____

Luke 12:29 – "And seek not ye what ye shall eat, or what ye shall drink, neither be ye of doubtful mind."

Write an affirmation of this scripture from your brand new Christ-Mind!

_____

_____

_____

_____

_____

I Corinthians 2:16 – "For who hath known the mind of the Lord, that he may instruct him? But we have the mind of Christ."

Write an affirmation of this scripture from your brand new Christ-Mind!

_____

_____

_____

_____

_____

Ephesians 4:17-23 – "This I say therefore, and testify in the Lord, that ye henceforth walk not as other Gentiles walk, in the vanity of their mind, Having the understanding darkened, being alienated from the life of God through the ignorance that is in them, because of the blindness of their heart: Who being past feeling have given themselves over unto lasciviousness, to work all uncleanness with greediness. But ye have not so learned Christ; If so be that ye have heard him, and have been taught by him, as the truth is in Jesus: That ye put off concerning the former conversation the old man, which is corrupt according to the deceitful lusts; And be renewed in the spirit of your mind;"

Write an affirmation of faith based on Ephesians 4:17-23 from your brand new Christ-Mind!

_____

_____

_____

_____

_____

_____

_____

Colossians 1:20-22 – "And, having made peace through the blood of his cross, by him to reconcile all things unto himself; by him, I say, whether they be things in earth, or things in heaven. And you, that were sometime alienated and enemies in your mind by wicked works, yet now hath he reconciled in the body of his flesh through death, to present you holy and unblameable and unreproveable in his sight:"

Write an affirmation of faith based on these scriptures from your new Christ-Mind!

_____

_____

_____

_____

_____

_____

_____

Colossians 3:1-14 – "If ye then be risen with Christ, seek those things which are above, where Christ sitteth on the right hand of God. Set your affection on things above, not on things on the earth. For ye are dead, and your life is hid with Christ in God When Christ, who is our life, shall appear, then shall ye also appear with him in glory. Mortify therefore your members which are upon the earth; fornication, uncleanness, inordinate affection, evil concupiscence, and covetousness, which is idolatry: For which things' sake the wrath of God cometh on the children of disobedience: In which ye also walked some time, when ye lived in them.   But now ye also put off all these; anger, wrath, malice, blasphemy, filthy communication out of your mouth.   Lie not one to another, seeing that ye have put off the old man with his deeds; And have put on the new man, which is renewed in knowledge after the image of him that created him: Where there is neither Greek nor Jew, circumcision nor uncircumcision, Barbarian, Scythian, bond nor free: but Christ is all, and in all. Put on therefore, as the elect of God, holy and beloved, bowels of mercies, kindness, humbleness of mind, meekness, longsuffering; Forbearing one another, and forgiving one another, if any man have a quarrel against any: even as Christ forgave you, so also do ye. And above all these things put on charity, which is the bond of perfectness."

Write an affirmation of faith based on these scriptures from your new Christ-Mind!

_____

_____

_____

_____

_____

_____

2 Timothy 1:6-8 – "Wherefore I put thee in remembrance that thou stir up the gift of God, which is in thee by the putting on of my hands. For God hath not given us the spirit of fear; but of power, and of love, and of a sound mind. Be not thou therefore ashamed of the testimony of our Lord, nor of me his prisoner: but be thou partaker of the afflictions of the gospel according to the power of God;"

Write an affirmation of faith based on these scriptures from your new Christ-Mind!

_____

_____

_____

_____

_____

_____

I Peter 1:13 – "Wherefore gird up the loins of your mind, be sober, and hope to the end for the grace that is to be brought unto you at the revelation of Jesus Christ;"

Write an affirmation of faith based on this scripture from your new Christ-Mind!

_____

_____

_____

_____

_____

_____

_____

James 1:1-8 – "James, a servant of God and of the Lord Jesus Christ, to the twelve tribes which are scattered abroad, greeting. My brethren, count it all joy when ye fall into divers temptations; knowing this, that the trying of your faith worketh patience. But let patience have her perfect work, that ye may be perfect and entire, wanting nothing. If any of you lack wisdom, let him ask of God, that giveth to all men liberally, and upbraideth not; and it shall be given him. But let him ask in faith, nothing wavering. For he that wavereth is like a wave of the sea driven with the wind and tossed. For let not that man think that he shall receive any thing of the Lord. A double minded man is unstable in all his ways."

Write an affirmation of faith based on these scriptures from your new Christ-Mind!

_____

_____

_____

_____

_____

_____

_____

_____

_____

_____

4.12 GO! HURRY! PICK UP YOUR PEARLS!

Matthew 7:6 – "Give not that which is holy unto the dogs, neither cast ye your pearls before swine, lest they trample them under their feet, and turn again and rend (*tear, mar, mall, injure, hurt*) you."

Perhaps, you were hurt in the past because you trusted, loved, served, needed, befriended or depended upon the wrong people! What valuable parts of who you are (pearls), including your intellect, knowledge, emotions, wisdom, etc., do you need to retrieve in the spirit from people who either didn't appreciate you or what you gave to them or both?

Spend some time in meditation about your pearls. This should take a while, and maybe more paper in your journal.   Make a simple declaration below that you now retrieve all of your pearls that were cast with the wrong people! GET EXCITED! SPEAK IT VERBALLY – OUT LOUD! TAKE THEM BACK! As you go forward, please be careful where and with whom you share costly spiritual, intellectual, emotional and even material treasures of your life.

_____

_____

_____

_____

CHANGE!
IT IS REQUIRED FOR CHRISTIANS!

Accept Jesus' Spiritual Healing!
I Peter 2:24 – "Who his own self bare our sins in his own body on the tree, that we, being dead to sins, should live unto righteousness: by whose stripes ye were healed."

Accelerate God's Deliverance Through Faith!
Matthew 6:13 – " And lead us not into temptation, but deliver us from evil: For thine is the kingdom, and the power, and the glory, for ever. Amen."

Activate God the Holy Spirit's Recovery!
I Samuel 30:8 – "And David enquired at the Lord, saying, Shall I pursue after this troop? Shall I overtake them? And he answered him, Pursue: for thou shalt surely overtake them, and without fail recover all."

God promises that you will recover everything that was taken from you. Change is required. Change from the caterpillar to the butterfly! Permit God the Holy Spirit to change you from carnal to spiritual; from mortal to immortality

5.0 – VICTORY!

5.1 – RAPTURE READINESS!

Ephesians 6:10-20

"Finally, my brethren, be strong in the Lord, and in the power of his might. Put on the whole armor of God, that ye may be able to stand against the wiles of the devil. For we wrestle not against flesh and blood, but against principalities, against powers, against the rulers of the darkness of this world, against spiritual wickedness in high places. Wherefore take unto you the whole armor of God that ye may be able to withstand in the evil day, and having done all, to stand. Stand therefore, having your loins girt about with truth, and having on the breastplate of righteousness; and your feet shod with the preparation of the gospel of peace; above all, taking the shield of faith, wherewith ye shall be able to quench all the fiery darts of the wicked. And take the helmet of salvation, and the sword of the Spirit, which is the word of God: Praying always with all prayer and supplication in the Spirit, and watching thereunto with all perseverance and supplication for all saints; and for me, that utterance may be given unto me, that I may open my mouth boldly, to make known the mystery of the gospel..."

Jesus already won the victory! The fight is fixed! We win! Just stand!
Thank You Jesus!
Smile!

5.2 – ARMORED FOR VICTORY!
Ephesians 6:10-24

Battle-Readiness Regalia

- Truth!

- Righteousness!

- Peace!

- Faith!

- Salvation!

- Word of God!

- Prayer!

- Zeal!

Dress for success! As you go forward in God the Holy Spirit, Who is present with you and in you, let this be the image of who you are, daily, in your imagination. Vision yourself as the child of God who is a Victorious Christian, in all things. Jesus already won at Calvary. IN JESUS CHRIST, we win in all things. We win over our hurt. VICTORY is ours. In Jesus Name! Jesus' Name is Amen, (Revelation 3:14) which means: It is so! So be it! Praise God even while you wait to see the manifestation of victory! Victory is assured!

Live life as the Victorious Christian who Christ saves and sets free!

5.3 – PURPOSE OF ARMOR!

2 Corinthians 10:3-4 – "For though we walk in the flesh, we do not war after the flesh; (For the weapons of our warfare are not carnal, but mighty through God to the pulling down of strong holds:) Casting down imaginations and every high thing that exalts itself against the knowledge of God, and bringing into captivity, every thought to the obedience of Christ;"

We first see Jesus through the eyes of the spirit in the Book of Joshua 5:13-15. He makes a Pre-Incarnate appearance. He steps through the space/time dimension before He enters the world as human in Bethlehem. This phenomenon is called a Christophany. As Joshua prepared to conquer Jericho to secure the Promised Land, Jesus stops by and presents Himself as a mighty warrior. He describes Himself as the Captain of the Host of the Lord.

The Book of Joshua is the Old Testament companion to the New Testament Book of Ephesians. In Joshua, the battle was real in the physical. In the New Testament Book of Ephesians, our battle is real, also, though it is spiritual. Ephesians teaches us how to war in the spirit. So, it is no wonder that Ephesians closes with the description of our armor for warfare. Study both Books, carefully.

It is true! The battle is the Lord's. However, we are required to prepare for war. We are required to show up on the battlefield – dressed, healed and whole, expecting to see God move on our behalf. We are the mighty Army of the Lord!

The scripture in 2 Corinthians 10:3-4 is clear. The battle is spiritual and must be handled spiritually. The flesh wars against the spirit. Your spirit must overcome the flesh and take authority over it and everything in your life through the power of God the Holy Spirit!

The purpose of the whole armor of God is to:

- Experience GOD in Three Persons – God the Father, Son, Holy Spirit!
- Get and keep our spirits, souls, and minds focused on Jesus and the victory at Calvary;
- Identify us as the soldiers in the Army of the Lord;
- Help us recognize each other – who are on the Lord's side;
- Use the Word of God as a skilled warrior;
- Take authority over the attacks of the enemy;
- Force demons to bow in the Presence of Jesus in you at the Name of Jesus;
- Realize now the victory at Calvary, the end-time victory and the incredible value of our personal relationship with God through Christ;
- Facilitate our ability to stand strong to see the salvation of the Lord; and
- Become whole and remain protected in Jesus Christ!

"Be strong in the Lord and in the power of his might..."

5.4 – THE LOIN ATTIRE OF TRUTH!

John 8:31-32 – "Then said Jesus to those Jews which believed on him, If ye continue in my word, then are ye my disciples indeed; And ye shall know the truth, and the truth shall make you free."

Have you ever considered the fact that the only clothes remaining on Jesus Christ, Who is the absolute Truth, as He hung on the cross, was a loincloth? The Truth that Jesus is the Son of God and all the other truths in the Word of God did not change, even as He died for us. In fact the Truth was made visible for the whole world to see throughout all ages and circumstances.

Visualize the Loin Cloth of Truth, daily. It is your ever-present covering of victory as the son or daughter of God. Know the Truth who is Christ. Permit nothing and no one to ever separate you from the love of God – The Truth. Nothing can separate God's love for you from God's side. Do not permit hurt, sin or anything else to come between you and God, from your side of the New Covenant. Keep wearing the attire of Truth to the end.

The Truth MAKES you free! You have God's Word on it!

5.5 – RIGHTEOUSNESS COVERING!

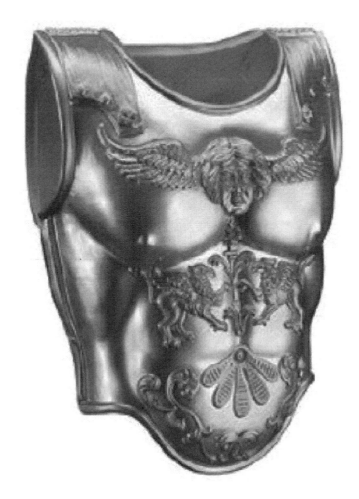

Covers:

- Heart

- Spirit

- Soul
  (Mind,
  Will,
  Emotions, &
  Imagination)

It is written:

I Peter 2:9 – "But ye are a chosen generation, a royal priesthood, an holy nation, a peculiar people; that ye should show forth the praises of him who hath called you out of darkness into his marvelous light;"

There is a strong spiritual relationship between the Ephod that the priests wore in the Old Testament and the Breastplate of Righteousness that God commands us to wear in Ephesians 6:14. The righteousness of God is our ascent to live blamelessly according to the Word of God in Christian virtue, honor, morality, and justice, as we bear the Fruit of the Spirit with hope to a sinful, dying world.

Every believing follower of Jesus Christ is called to wear the Ephod of the Royal Priesthood that is the Breastplate of Righteousness. It is our protection against the assault of the enemy. It guards us against the seduction of evil. It is the critical covering for the life giving and sustaining flow of the Blood of Christ; and the Wind and Fire of God the Holy Spirit to our spirit, souls, bodies, and minds.

5.6 – GOSPEL OF THE PREPARATION OF PEACE!

Joshua 1:3 – "Every place that the sole of your foot shall tread upon, that have I given unto you, as I said unto Moses."

Ephesians 6:14-15 – "Stand therefore, having your loins girt about with truth, and having on the breastplate of righteousness; and your feet shod with the preparation of the gospel of peace:"

In Joshua 1:3, God makes a promise of victory to Joshua as soon as he accepts the leadership role for the Israelites, after the death of Moses. God uses the "SOLE of the foot" of Joshua on the move to make the promise.

We see the image of the gladiator's shoes above. Yet, God commands us to shod our feet with peace. The instruction is to nail peace to our feet as one would the shoe to a horse. The "preparation of the gospel of peace" says to us to prepare for battle with the Good News of the peace which surpasses all understanding". It is possible when we understand Jesus is the Commander in Chief of our lives. We prepare for a war that we will not fight BECAUSE we stand in the spirit of peace, and the power of God the Holy Spirit.

On the surface, it would seem to be a contradiction of war to stand in peace. However, the results are in the hand of God who has already accomplished the victory. Jericho fell without a fight, just a shout! Walk the Christ-Walk IN God's promises in peace! SHOUT!

5.7 – SHIELD OF FAITH!

How strong
is your shield?

As substance,
faith assumes the
holy character,
POWER, and quality
of the need.

Your shield of faith
covers you and
others.

The more the shield
is tested the stronger
it is and becomes.

Master the skills to
manage your OWN
Shield of Faith.

Initial Acts of Faith to Win!

Standing Faith	Waiting Faith
Walking Faith	Expectant Faith
Running Faith	Changing Faith
Overcoming Faith	Healing Faith

According to 2 Timothy 1:7, God has not given us the spirit of fear. Fear is the fuel that lights the fiery darts of the enemy. The Shield of Faith is the power of God to extinguish them. Remember! Through Christ Jesus, "You are more than a conqueror." Beloved! You are a WINNER!

5.8 – HELMET OF SALVATION!

GOD'S FORTIFIED COVERING FOR VICTORIOUS LIFE NOW AND ETERNAL LIFE TO COME!

Ephesians 2:8-9 – "For by grace are ye saved through faith: and that not of ourselves: it is the gift of God: Not of works, lest any man should boast."

Salvation (Soteria) is the all-encompassing act of Jesus on the cross. By His grace through our faith, everything about us and that concerns us is saved through the Blood of the Lamb of God – Jesus Christ. The Helmet of Salvation protects the head where God reveal's God's will to us. God's Helmet of Salvation protects:

- Our Purpose – Worship God! Focus!
- Our Thoughts – Think the thoughts of God with the Christ-Mind!
- Our Imagination – See what God reveals beyond what is seen in the natural!
- Our Visioning – Embellish what God reveals through additional revelations!
- Our Goals – Process with Christ how to accomplish the will of God!
- Our Decisions – Choose to do the will of God, God's way! Always!
- Actions – Spiritually energize God's revelations to accomplish all things through Christ!

KEEP THE HELMET OF SALVATION UP STRAIGHT ON YOUR HEAD!

5.9 – SWORD OF THE SPIRIT!

Matthew 4:4 – "But he answered and said, It is written, Man shall not live by bread alone, but by every word that proceeds out of the mouth of God."

John 1:1-14 – "In the beginning was the Word, and the Word was with God, and the Word was God. The same was in the beginning with God... And the Word was made flesh, and dwelt among us, (and we beheld his glory, the glory as of the only begotten of the Father) full of grace and truth."

Hebrews 4:12 – "For the word of God is quick, and powerful, and sharper than any two-edged sword, piercing even to the dividing asunder of soul and spirit, and of the joints and marrow, and is a discerner of the thoughts and intents of the heart."

Have you ever considered how eternal and ancient is this Sword – The Word of God? How tried and true is its power! Have you ever imagined and embraced the truth that the Word of God is God made flesh to live among us and in us?

The Word of God is prescriptive. It is the life-giving medicine for every hurt that we feel or ever encountered. Everything you need for life and life everlasting is written in the Word of God! The Word of God is prevention against the wiles, attempts, and attacks, tricks and traps of the enemy. The Word of God is power that God adds to our lives when we believe the Word. THE WORD JUST IS BECAUSE GOD IS!

When we are the most vulnerable, we must "only believe" with the last mustard seed of faith that remains. Faith worked works faith. Like a loving parent, God hears your cry. God promises to show God strong on your behalf. God is near – as close as the Word in your mouth. Speak the Word. Let the following commands be your mantra for healing, deliverance, and recovery to go forward in all things. Hang the Word about your neck that you may stand each day in the power of God.

- "Have faith in God!" (Mark 11:22)

- "Be not afraid!" (Mark 5:36)

- "Only believe!" (Mark 5:36)

- "Jesus!" Speak His Name! (Mark 16:17-18; John 14:12-15; Acts 3:16)

5.10 – TWO MORE SPIRITUAL WEAPONS!

PRAYER!

Ephesians 6:18-19 – "Praying always with all prayer and supplication in the Spirit, and watching thereunto with all perseverance and supplication for all saints; And for me, that utterance may be given unto me, that I may open my mouth boldly, to make known the mystery of the gospel..."

Prayer is a vital weapon to transform us; prevent the assault of the enemy; experience healing for us; and to minister healing to others. Jesus prayed for us, even as He prepared to die for us. In many ways, John 17 is Jesus prayer covering for us – that we would be one with Him. If we are one with Him, we are whole. We are victorious!

THE BLOOD OF JESUS!

Exodus 24:8 – "And Moses took the blood, and sprinkled it on the people and said, behold the blood of the covenant which the Lord hath made with you concerning all these words."

Revelation 5:6 – "And I beheld, and, lo, in the midst of the throne and of the four beasts, and in the midst of the elders, stood a Lamb as it had been slain, having seven horns and seven eyes, which are the seven Spirits of God sent forth into all the earth."

In our Old Testament example, Moses sprinkled the people with the blood of animals, to affirm the Covenant of God with God's people. In the New Testament, the Blood of Jesus was shed for us for the remission of our sins and as a seal of the New Covenant that Jesus makes available to anyone and everyone! The Blood of Jesus redeemed us (bought us back) and saves us.

The image of the scourged canals on Jesus' body that flowed with His Blood from the 39 stripes He received for our healing should be seared in our minds, our hearts, and our souls, lest in times of trouble, we forget His sacrifice. Jesus was wounded from the crown of His head to the soles of His feet. The image reminds us that through the salvation of Jesus Christ, His wounds HEALED US from the crown of our heads to the soles of our feet – our spirits, souls, minds, and bodies.

We pray and believe to see the reality of that healing in our daily lives. By faith, we diligently work to love God with all our hearts, souls and minds before we see the reality of the things for which we hoped.

The language used in Revelation 5:6 presents Jesus as the Lamb whose Blood is still flowing to the end of all times. There is power in The Blood.

We are in THE BLOODLINE of Jesus Christ – healed and whole!

5.11 – ETERNAL LIFE!

1 Thessalonians 4:15-17 – "For this we say unto you by the word of the Lord, that we which are alive and remain unto the coming of the Lord shall not prevent them which are asleep. For the Lord himself shall descend from heaven with a shout, with the voice of the archangel, and with the trump of God: and the dead in Christ shall rise first: Then we which are alive and remain shall be caught up together with them in the clouds, to meet the Lord in the air: and so shall we ever be with the Lord."

Fear not! God promised. Know what God says in the Holy Bible and "faith it" through. Get with and remain in the Presence of the God of Jesus Christ. Eternal life is really not about religion – a set of rules, events, entertainment, behavior and just stuff that humans created. It is all about our relationship with God through the Messiah – Jesus Christ. The Son of God gave His life to restore and secure blessedness for anyone who believes that Jesus is the Son of God; and that God raised Jesus from the dead. You are saved! And so...

Remember! Eternal life begins NOW! It requires that we love God with all our heart, souls, and minds, NOW. It is possible. Jesus commanded it. God the Holy Spirit helps us obey! ETERNAL LIFE BEGINS WITH SALVATION. Salvation is a process of change. Love God with all your heart, soul, and mind. God's love for you is transformational. Love God back. Love yourself. Love others!

If I miss you down here, we'll see each other in the Rapture!
WE LOVE YOU IN CHRIST...BECAUSE OF CHRIST...BY HIS GRACE!

Jude :3
...""earnestly contend for the faith that was once delivered to the saints.""

5.12 – NEXT STEP!

Beloved:

All praises to our God and King! Thank you for your outstanding discipline to complete the **Heal the Hurt! Live the Victory** Seminar I and **The Workbook**. We are praying for you and your coninued recovery and growth in the Lord Jesus Christ! You are now prepared for **Seminar II: Heal the Hurt: Live the Victory: 12 Keys to Spiritual Deliverance and Recovery!**

When requirements for Seminars I and II are completed, you will be eligible for the Institute for Christian Disicpleship, Inc. to certify you as a Life Guardian.   Remember Jesus' instruction to Peter in Luke 22:31-32. When we are converted, when we are changed, Jesus commands us to strengthen, to edify, to build up other believers.

Thank you for sharing the news about our Seminars and this Workbook! Please contact the Institute for Christian Discipleship, Inc. for updates on seminars near you.   We will also inform you about how you may receive The Workbook and PowerPoint presentation for Seminar II, so that you may engage in independent study when it is available.

We are grateful for your obedience to God's command to "earnestly contend for the faith that was once delivered to the saints". We look forward to sharing our ministry with you in the future. We pray God's abundance in every area of your life. God will work through you to make a difference in the lives of of others because of your faithfulness and courage to change. Please be patient with yourself, God, and others as the change takes place.

I offer a special thanks to God for all the victorious students since 1992.   I love you greatly! Because of the evidence of God's healing and wholeness in your life, you yet inspire me to do more to help God heal God's people.

Grace and Peace,
Pastor Nawanna Lewis Miller – B.A., M.A., M.Div

"….by His grace…"

BENEDICTUS!

JUDE 1:20-25

"But ye, beloved, building up yourselves on your most holy faith, praying in the Holy Ghost, Keep yourselves in the love of God, looking for the mercy of our Lord Jesus Christ unto eternal life. And of some have compassion, making a difference: And others save with fear, pulling them out of the fire; hating even the garment spotted by the flesh."

"Now unto him that is able to keep you from falling, and to present you faultless before the presence of his glory with exceeding joy, to the only wise God our Savior, be glory and majesty, dominion and power, both now and ever. Amen."

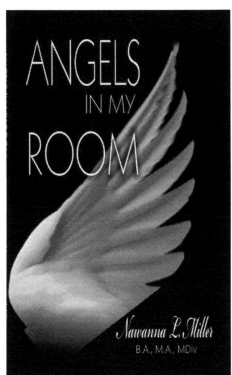

Angels in My Room
By: Nawanna Lewis Miller

$14.00 – Plus $4.000 Tax/Shipping/ Handling

Angels in My Room provides a frame of reference through which we look to see the picture that God presents regarding God's healing power working through people for people or ourselves. God charges believers in Jesus Christ with the responsibility to heal and use the Gifts of Healing for others.

If you are Christian, healing is a part of your ministry of discipleship. Christians have the authority to exercise faith in healing as a reality of our call to discipleship. If you are reading this writing, there is a 100% chance that you are called to be one of God's "angels in the room".

We are on assignment. We are called to be messengers, who use the gifts of God the Holy Spirit to minister healing, wherever healing is needed – physical, spiritual, emotional, and relational healing. The room is the space that those who will receive healing occupy – as remote as a battlefield; as intimate as a chair in the bedroom; or as public as a street corner or restaurant. This book tells you the basics – the who, what, when, where, and how of healing!

Cruising the Cosmos
(Meditations via God the Holy Spirit)

To step away from the noise and the crowds, to be alone with God and the thoughts that God thinks toward us and we think toward God is what **Cruising the Cosmos (World)** is all about. It is a book of meditations, generated through contemplations and visioning with God the Holy Spirit. Some of the meditations are poetic with rhythm and rhyme. Others are sermonic prose or metaphoric narratives. Still others are simple musings with God!

All of the compilations are instructive to inspire the reader to think of God's enormous, unlimited and eternal love toward us. When we go to the end of our knowing, we find God with us, to provide fresh revelation of God our Divine Creator. The God of Jesus Christ yet desires to cruise the cosmos with us. The still, small voice of God says: "Lo, I am with you always, even to the end of the world (cosmos)".

For publications, please visit us @www.proofpositivebooks.com

Please Like Us: Proof Positive Communications@Facebookpages.com
Institute for Christian Discipleship, Inc.@Facebookpages.com

Reverend Nawanna Lewis Miller - B.A., M.A., M.Div.

Reverend Nawanna Lewis Miller is a life-long Christian who celebrates the memory of her first encounter with Jesus Christ while she was yet in a high chair. Throughout her life, she has vigorously served in the church of Jesus Christ. God the Holy Spirit continues to give her prophetic vision and revelation to expand the scope of work to which God assigns her hands.

She is married to her high school sweetheart, George C, Miller, Jr.! Together, they serve God as parents to five children, and four grandchildren. She always lives on the premise that her first ministry for God is to her family – her husband, children, grandchildren, and progeny yet unborn. She does not deviate from that practice. She is the daughter of these citizens of heaven – John and Thelma Lewis; and George and Beatrice Miller. She shares the journey with one brother , four sisters, neices, nephews, the faimily of God and many friends.

Metropolitan Baptist Church in Washinton, D.C., under the pastorate of Reverend Dr. H. Hcks, Jr., licensed her in 1989. On May 17, 1992, a host of phenomenal clergy ordained her to the gospel ministry there, following a substantial public catechism with over 1,000 people in attendance. Highly esteemed clergy courageously ordained a preacher who was female, when to do so was yet contested in the Baptist denomination.

Reverend Miller is a graduate of H.M. Turner High School in Atlanta, Georgia. She is one of the early African-American graduates of the University of Georgia in Athens, Georgia where she earned the ABJ degree in Broadcast Journalism. The Master of Arts in Organizational Communications was earned at the Howard University Graduate School of Arts and Sciences. The Master of Divinity Degree was earned at the Howard University School of Divinity.

God permits her to serve as the Founding Pastor of the Messiah's Temple Christian Ministries in Austell, Georgia since 1995; Founder and Leading Director of The Institute for Christian Discipleship, Inc. since 1995; Founding Chairperson and President of Hannah's Hope Family Life Center, Inc., a Nonprofit 501(C)3 Corporation since 1999; and Founding President and Chairperson of Proof Positive Communications, Inc., since 1981.

She is the author of three books: **Angels in My Room; Cruising the Cosmos**; and **Heal the Hurt: Live the Victory!** Reverend Miller is the personal pastor and counsellor to countless people across the country, from all walks of life, including clergy and leaders. She walks with people on the journey as a Bible-basd spirutal pastor, teacher, and trusted friend.

Τετέλεσται!
"It... is... finished!"
JESUS!

Made in the
USA
Lexington, KY